ERRATA

Page 21 - 3rd paragraph 3rd sentence, the correct word is "increased," not "reduced."

page 57 - Caption - the correct spelling is Sarepta

Page 67 - 2nd paragraph, line 3, the correct elevation is 2000 feet, not 200.

Aviation's Quiet Pioneer

John Leslie

by Peter Leslie

John Leslie's Pan American Airways service pins for 25 and 40 years

©Copyright 2011 Peter Leslie
All rights reserved

Leslie's 3 year service pin

CONTENTS

FOREWORD		5
CHAPTER 1	PIONEERS, SOD HUT AND OXCART	6
	"ARE YOU A LESLIE STANDARD?"	8
	ARCHEOLOGY AND AERONAUTICS	10
CHAPTER 2 -	FIRST JOB, FIRST IMPRESSIONS AND MOONLIGHT CRUISES	13
	A FLYING HONEYMOON	16
	FIRST SLOAN SCHOLAR AT MIT	21
CHAPTER 3	"FATHER OF LONG RANGE CRUISING"	24
	"HOW LONG CAN THIS SHIP STAY IN THE AIR?"	30
	TAKING DELIVERY OF THE *CHINA CLIPPER*	38
CHAPTER 4	"I THRILL TO THE WONDER OF IT ALL"	40
	"MAKE MEN AND MACHINES WORK TOGETHER"	45
	"TO OUR UTTER SADNESS"	51
CHAPTER 5	"A MOST SHOCKING AND INCREDIBLE MYSTERY"	57
	THE MIGHTY, MARVELOUS BOEING 314	63
	"THERE'S YOUR LAND, BOYS"	66
CHAPTER 6	"IT ALL SEEMS UTTERLY INSANE"	69
	"1935 - 1941 WERE GOLDEN"	71
	"MY NEW DIVISION WAS AT WAR"	72
CHAPTER 7	"NO BUZZ-BOMB FOUND ME THAT NIGHT"	80
	"WE ARE ALL FIGHTING WITH ONE MIND AND HEART"	84
	"WIN THE WAR AND THE FUTURE!"	89
EPILOGUE		91
AFTERWORD		99

Dedicated to the memory of those who lost their lives in the pioneering days of transoceanic flight and in recognition of all members of the Pan Am family who participated in creating a great airline.

A Sikorsky S-42 crossing the ocean, by Clayton Knight

FOREWORD

The air was not conquered by the invention of the flying machine but by the development of the invention for use; this development involved the improvement and adaptation of materiel, the organization of ground services, relations with governments, financing and all the rest of the complicated and innumerable activities necessary to put planes in the air and bring them down again — and Pan American, in all of these activities, was the pioneer.

It was a corporation capable, as few corporations ever have been, of dreaming. And what it dreamed of was a sea which would unite mankind rather than divide it as the waters for so long had done — a sea of air.

Archibald MacLeish, American poet, writer, Pulitzer Prize winner, Librarian of Congress......from a 1971 letter.

In 1929, John C. Leslie, MIT trained aeronautical engineer, was hired by Pan American Airways in New York as assistant to Chief Engineer Andre Priester. He was soon posted to Miami where Pan American was rapidly expanding its routes and buying new flying machines, both flying boats and landplanes.

In 1935, Leslie was Division Engineer when the Pacific Ocean was spanned by Pan American's majestic flying boat, the *China Clipper*. The legendary Captain Ed Musick was in command of the crew of seven. The take off was carried live on national radio. Tens of thousands watched along the shores of San Francisco Bay.

To cross the Pacific carrying a payload was an historic event. America and the world marveled at its technical audacity. Its speed was considered miraculous; it took only five days flying, four nights ashore and 59 hours in the air. TIME magazine put Musick's photograph on the cover. FORTUNE featured the plane and Pan American's string of island bases. Pan American's founder, visionary entrepreneur and aviator, Juan Trippe, was lionized across America and beyond.

When my father died in 1982, the New York Times described him as a pioneer of the technology of over-ocean flight. He worked with Lindbergh, Sikorsky, Martin and with many others who dedicated their lives to challenging the outer boundaries of technology. Their goal was to link the world so that passengers and goods could be carried ever faster and ever more economically. They achieved that goal. I believe my father would say, "I was just one member of a great team."

When I undertook this book I had file boxes containing my father's papers, memorabilia, unpublished memoirs, photo albums, and his collection of aviation books. I restricted myself principally to these materials to let his voice, those of his contemporaries, and historians tell his story, a story shared in so many ways by every member of the Pan Am team across more than six decades.

Peter Leslie

CHAPTER 1
PIONEERS, SOD HUT AND OXCART

John C. Leslie was the fourth son of a prosperous Minneapolis family, but he was born not far in time from a sod hut in the Dakota Territories and a cobbler's shop in a little town in Ireland.

His grandparents, James and Mary Ann Leslie, in 1878 abandoned their grocery and shoemaker's trade in Ballybay, County Monaghan, and, in the wake of famine and religious strife, emigrated to America. They left behind James' aged mother and their eldest son, John Leslie, who had been apprenticed to a printer for four years. That printer had become John's legal father under the terms of the standard apprenticeship contract of those days. Mary Ann was convinced she would never see her son again.

James and Mary Ann Leslie in Ireland

James patented 80 acres near what is now Mitchell, South Dakota, and started a farm where none had existed before. Patenting land under the Homestead Act gave immigrants government land, provided they agreed to farm it for a number of years. The land had been occupied by the Sioux Indians who still roamed the plains.

Excerpt from a letter from one of James and Mary Ann's great-granddaughters

```
                                            Mother told about
the yearly fall trek to Yankton to get sugar, flour,
salt, lumber, and supplies to last through the winter,
She said it took about three weeks.to make the trip
by oxen at first and later they had horses.
```

First they lived in a sod hut on the plains, which was an extremely primitive existence even by 19th century standards. Later they built a small wooden house. James walked six miles each way six days a week to work in a mill in Mitchell, South Dakota. Yearly they travelled by oxcart to Yankton for supplies. Just the traveling 100 miles took a week each way, a journey that today would take less than two hours.

In 1890 James and Mary Ann experienced a terrible loss in a diphtheria epidemic. Their four youngest children died along with two grandchildren. Before they left Ireland two other sons had died at ages two and fourteen of unrecorded causes. Out of eleven children, five survived to adulthood.

Their great-granddaughter, Ann Leslie McCarthy, wrote about this tragedy and their hard life in her 1982 family history, **From Ballybay to the USA**.

Standing as I did on the farm looking up at the burial plot above the edge of the river bed it was easy to feel the deep heartbreak of the father who had to carry the young, lifeless bodies up the bank to bury them in the hard, cold ground. He surely must have felt that God was punishing him for his earlier rebellion. God's wrath had caught up with him and delivered this dreadful punishment. It was almost beyond endurance, and the effect lingered with him the rest of his life. James Leslie never recovered from this great loss and died in Minneapolis in 1899 of 'exhaustion,' according to his death certificate.

All of his life James Leslie had known hardship. Famine, drought, hard work, harsh conditions demanding everything he had to give were his lot in life. His boys were exposed to many of the same conditions. By giving them the new opportunities of a fresh start and the discipline to achieve their goals, James Leslie gave his family the greatest gift they could have asked for.

How I wish my great-grandfather could have sat beside me on the plane when we flew last summer out of Sioux Falls and passed over the Mitchell area. Looking down from thirty thousand feet I could see the extent of man's handiwork in the neatly cultivated, lush sections of land that have become part of the breadbasket of the world. Envisioning how it might have looked a hundred years before, wild, desolate, overwhelming in its vastness, I could appreciate the courage and tenacity of our ancestor. It would be comforting to know that this gallant man had an inkling of the success of his venture and the great gift he gave to generations of his family to come.

Monument at Mitchell, South Dakota, with the names of the four Leslie children who perished in the terrible epidemic. Their ages ranged from 9 to 16 years. The two grandchildren's names are on the other side; both were infants. The monument has tilted over the more than 120 years, but can still be read in spite of the years of wind, rain and snow.

"ARE YOU A LESLIE STANDARD?"

In 1880 John Leslie completed his apprenticeship and went to Dublin where he got a job in a book and stationery store. To keep up with his customers he read every book he could get his hands on. He was a bright, hardworking young man who assimilated the cultivated accent for which educated Dubliners are famous. When he decided to rejoin his family in the USA, he was running a store in Dungarvan for an absentee owner and may have been seeing a young woman, as family archives contain a picture of the two in nearby County Cork, but then she appears no more.

John Leslie and his son, John C. Leslie, circa 1912

SS Britannic in New York by Ian Marshall

John sailed from Ireland to New York in steerage class on the *SS Britannic*, a combination sailing and steam vessel. He arrived in New York in the summer of 1884 and took the train to Yankton, South Dakota, the end of the line. He spent a short time farming on the plains, decided he was better suited for being a merchant or a printer, and moved to Minneapolis, the booming city of what was then called the Northwest. John's first task was to find a job so he called on the biggest printer in the city. The owner asked him to proofread a text and John found three more errors than the owner, who immediately said, "You're hired." Some years later John met a pretty, Canadian emigrée, Bessie Mae McAfee, and asked her to marry him. Her uncle was so impressed with this ambitious, hardworking, young man he suggested they start a paper merchant firm, which they did in 1894. Leslie & McAfee prospered and John and Bessie Mae's marriage produced three sons, one after the other.

Eight years after the third boy was born, John Charles Leslie, future aviation pioneer, was a surprise arrival in 1905.

John Leslie was convinced that education was the key to getting ahead in America, so, at some financial sacrifice, he sent his three sons to Princeton University in New Jersey. He perceived that there were social advantages to attending well-known Eastern schools. When young John came along he was dispatched to the rigorous Phillips Exeter Academy in New Hampshire and then also to Princeton.

A man of both energy and ambition, he joined the Scottish Rite Masons, rising to the 33rd degree, became a leader in the Methodist Church and was active in politics. Young John once heard him chiding a fellow Irish immigrant about his accent from the old country, saying, "Sam, lose your accent! We are Americans now and we are here to stay." Apparently he had been willing to change his own accent for the second time.

For all his achievements in business, the Masons, the church, and politics, and while newspapers of the period hailed him as a key civic leader, he was not invited to join the Minneapolis Club. It was a subtle rebuke akin to the signs John saw in New York when he arrived in America: 'No Irish Need Apply.' He was heard to joke that, "Heck, I wouldn't want to join that club anyway. You go into the men's room there and the members are so old half can't start and the other half can't stop." Nonetheless, he attended a dinner there with 100 civic leaders and pledged the full share of $5,000 for a new building for the Minneapolis Institute of Arts, over $110,000 in 2010 dollars. It is not known if he was ever accepted into the club.

When Mr. McAfee died, the firm was renamed The John Leslie Paper Company. The company became well known and widely respected. John Leslie was elected president of the National Paper Trade Association. The company's sales manual, written circa 1900, is dedicated to the principles that hard work, honesty, clean living, and fair dealing inevitably lead to success. The company led the trend to uniform paper quality that printers could count on. This led to the creation of the term 'bond paper.' A principal product was 'Leslie Standard' and salesmen were urged to ask themselves each day, "Am I a Leslie Standard?"

Led by the young man who came to this country from Ireland and made his way without education or influence except a thorough training in the paper business, to the front rank among paper merchants of the United States, our Company has set a standard for you.

Do you represent The John Leslie Paper Company? Are you a "Leslie Standard?"

ARCHEOLOGY AND AERONAUTICS

John Charles Leslie was imbued with his father's spirit of hard work and high standards, but a chance event led him to a career in aviation. When he was fifteen, a barnstorming pilot was giving rides for $10 in a single engine amphibian near their home on Lake Minnetonka. That $10 would equal $109 in 2010 dollars. His father gave him the money and young John was hooked. He began dreaming about a a career in aviation, not paper. Although his father hoped he would become an engineer and join the family business, he generously said, "Of course, John, go ahead, but be sure to do it well."

John wrote in his memoirs, "If I was going to study engineering at MIT, I thought I had better go to the opposite extreme at Princeton. There I majored in Art and Archeology feeling this would be a painless way to study history, and indeed it was." He wrote a two volume monograph on the art and architecture of the ancient world. These contain hundreds of his sketches, such as the ones shown here, and from them one can see he had a gift for drawing and sketching, but, more important, a sense of structure and design. He graduated with high honors in 1926.

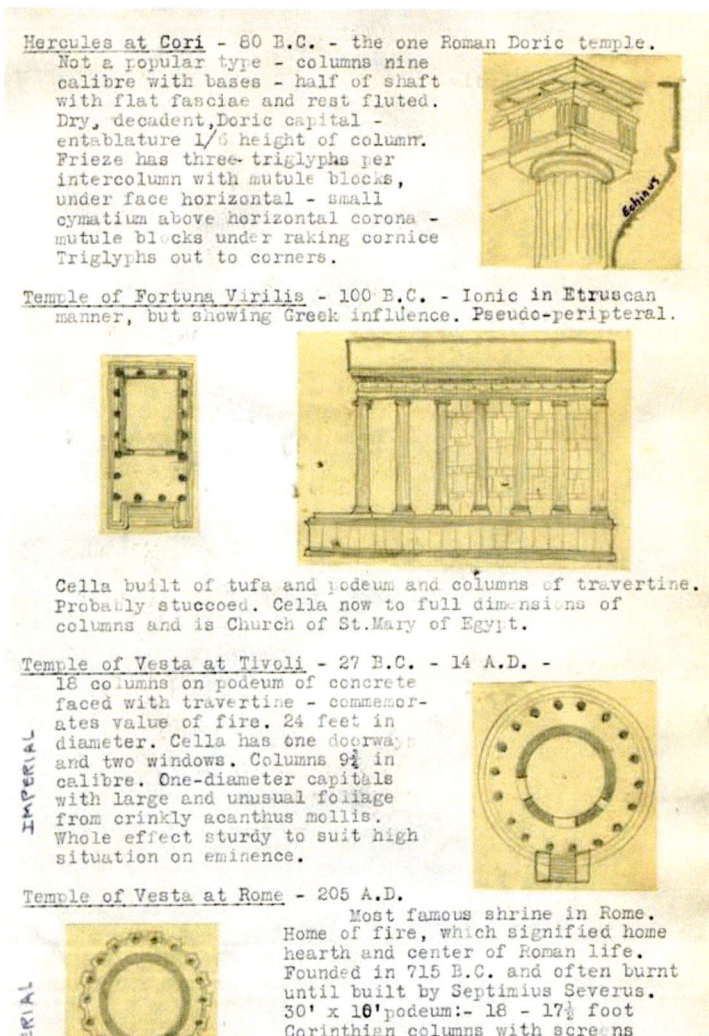

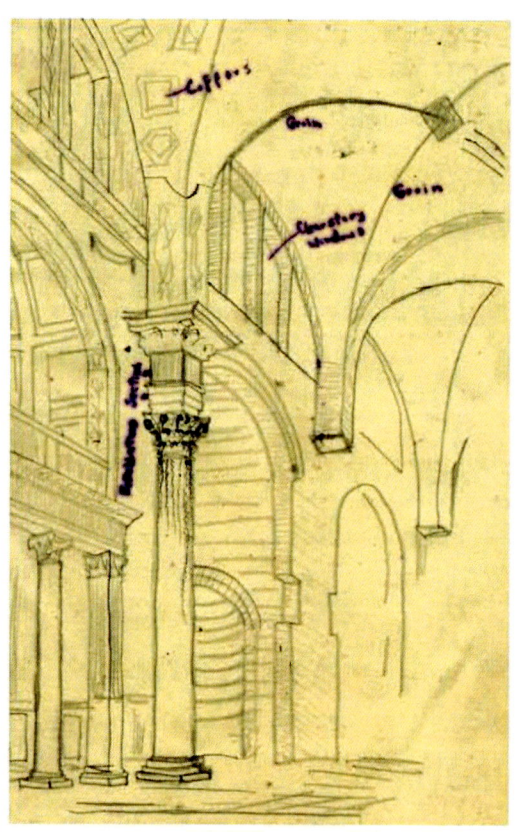

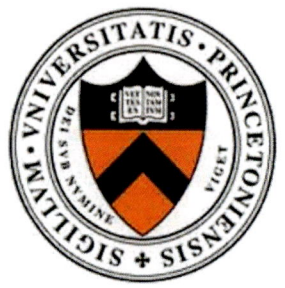

After Princeton, John went to Massachusetts Institute of Technology - (MIT), and in two years earned a B.S. in Aeronautical Engineering. He earned good marks and, among many other courses, designed the two-seater training plane shown below. In later years, he would explain that in 1928 not that much was known about the subject so, with the benefit of some technical courses at college, he was quickly able to satisfy the MIT requirements. He took every course they offered on the subject.

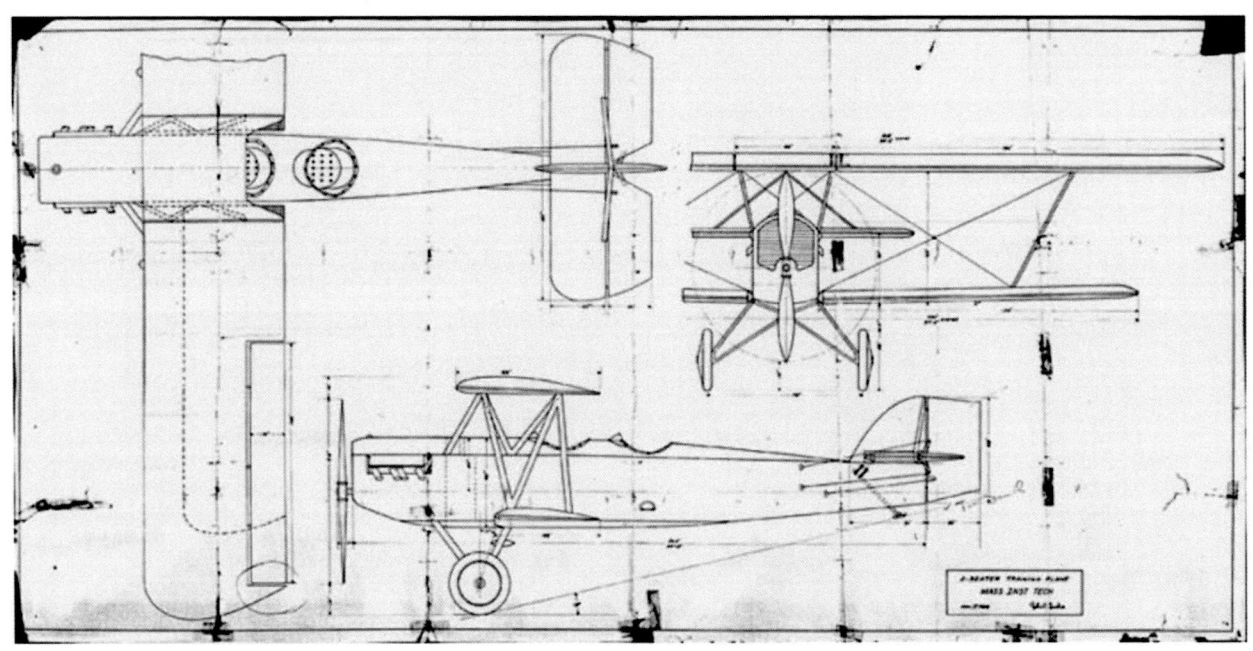

He did, however, say this about himself in his memoirs:

To be perfectly honest, I was not a very good engineer and would never have prospered at the design end of the business. I simply was not a good mathematician, did not have the abstract interests of a scientist, but did have sufficient talent to learn what I needed for the engineering and maintenance side of the airline business. I felt at home with the machinery, could understand the systems, and could also understand the more elevated discourse of the factory engineers.

Perhaps he was selling himself short because, just six years later, in 1934, he would work with Igor Sikorsky and other pioneers to create the technology and techniques of long-range transoceanic flight that successfully spanned the Pacific Ocean.

John photographed these barnstormers at the Minneapolis Airport, then a grass field.

Buhl Biplane with Wright J-5 "Whirlwind".

In 1927 Captain Ed Musick flew a Fokker F-10 on the first airmail flight from Havana, Cuba, to Key West, Florida. Leslie was still at MIT studying aeronautical engineering; Musick was ten years older than Leslie. They would work together closely starting in 1929.

John's first car.

Dad gave this to John in October, 1928 – his first car.

CHAPTER 4
FIRST JOB, FIRST IMPRESSIONS AND MOONLIGHT CRUISES

Fokker F-10 ready for delivery to Pan American

Right out of MIT in 1928, Leslie went to work as assistant to the famous Dutch airplane designer, Tony Fokker. His duties were vague and unpredictable. His memoirs indicate that Mr. Fokker kept irregular hours and that sometimes he would call Leslie to come to his home in the evening and be his clerk typist and editor. Fokker would hand a letter across the table and say, "Tell the S.O.B. No!" Leslie would type a more diplomatic note, which Fokker would sign. Realizing he had asked for far too small a salary when he was hired, he prepared a salary increase authorization and put it in the pile of letters and documents requiring Fokker's signature. When that came to the top of the pile, Fokker looked at him across the table, swore, "Well I'll be damned!" and signed it.

He did not stay with Fokker long because he decided he wanted to work for one of the pioneering airlines rather than a manufacturer. One day another Dutchman, Andre Priester, Pan American's Chief Engineer, came to the Fokker factory and met John Leslie for the first time. Soon thereafter he got an offer to work for Pan Am in New York, providing Mr. Fokker would not be annoyed. After working out a congenial transition, John accepted the job as assistant to the formidable Chief Engineer. He was quickly put to work inspecting and accepting new planes. In early 1929 Ed Musick, Pan Am's legendary Chief Pilot, was at the controls of one of those flights. Over the years they became close friends and worked together on developing the techniques for long range transoceanic flight, culminating in the flight of the famous *China Clipper*.

Leslie kept the flight log seen on the next page, which shows not only that first flight in 1920, but also the flights in which he was inspecting and problem solving.

The 1928 flights seen above were while he was working for Fokker. The 1929 flights were in the employ of Pan Am and involved accepting planes from Sikorsky, Fokker and Ford. His log shows 5 flights and 7 hours for 1928 and 39 flights and 26 hours for 1929.

This single log entry above shows Leslie's only crash. He was flying in an S-38 on an acceptance flight with a Sikorsky company pilot at the controls.

Leslie recalled in a speech at Phillips Exeter Academy in 1972:

I suppose no story of aeronautical adventure is complete without at least one mishap. Fortunately, I have experienced only one and the incident is recorded in a letter dated May 23, 1929, from the Sikorsky Aviation Corporation to the President of Pan Am. I quote the following excerpt:

'**.........from the photographs enclosed it seems almost incredible that this ship could take such a beating without the passengers sustaining serious injury. Apparently the damage to the plane itself is confined almost 100% to the struts and their fittings, all of which were more or less strained by the sudden stoppage of the amphibian when it finally came to an abrupt stop in the last ditch...**'

Leslie continues:

What happened was that the pilot landed the S-38 amphibian going too fast in the middle of a too-small field. He applied the power to the two engines, and one of them would not catch. Finally he pulled back the throttle on the operating engine, and from there we headed straight toward the 18th green of the adjoining golf course. We hit the first bunker, bounced up in the air, and put our tail skid down exactly in the hole, rolled across the green and down a steep grass wall into quite a deep bunker. At that point, the whole upper wing and the two engines all 'scrunched' forward two or three feet, fortunately not collapsing on top of us.

When John turned up after the crash his fiancée, Jean, noticed he was a bit woozy and not quite himself. In fact, he had suffered a mild concussion. This was just twelve days before their wedding.

Jean Savage was also from Lake Minnetonka and both families joked that it was a "mixed marriage." The Savages were all keen sailors and John had come courting in his father's elegant power boat. He overcame the initial "bad impression" several moonlight cruises later. To a certain extent Jean was the girl-next-door, as the families had known each other for years. His father had nominated her grandfather to be Governor of Minnesota, unsuccessfully as it turned out.

Family and friends gathered in Princeton where they were married on May 23, 1929, at the University Chapel. After a three-day honeymoon John went back to work in New York City. Mr. Priester needed him for urgent projects, delaying a proper honeymoon until later.

The Leslie-Savage wedding party

A FLYING HONEYMOON

At the end of 1929, Leslie was transferred to Miami where he was given the added responsibilities of Assistant Division Engineer. Leslie's initial duties involved maintaining the Consolidated Commodores acquired from The New York, Rio and Buenos Aires Airways — NYRBA, and testing new aircraft.

Consolidated Commodore

In mid 1930 Priester awarded Jean and John two round trip passes to Trinidad on the Fokker F-10's and the Sikorsky S-38's. They stopped at all the Pan American bases along the way. The trip was Mr. Priester's way of making up for having asked them earlier to cancel their honeymoon due to urgent airline business.

Their photograph album of this trip with pilots who later went on to Pacific crossing fame is a witness to early aviation, its equipment, its people, and primitive operating environment.

Notice how they dressed for travel; Jean wearing a corsage and John wearing snazzy two-tone shoes.

Early Pan American pilots, including Ed Musick and Leo Terletzky

Swinson - Musick - Schultz - Terletzky

Fokker F-10 at Havana, Cuba

Sikorsky S-38 Amphibian

Jean and John Leslie amid the struts of the S-38

Stuck in the mud at Santo Domingo

Captain Tilton signs the ship's papers and clears customs, St. Thomas, Virgin Islands

S-38 beached for the night before making a water take off at dawn.

Leslie's career had a dramatic hiccup five months after the honeymoon trip, but in his memoirs he made it sound like a lucky break.

He was sent to Belem do Pará, Brazil, with the expectation that he would be named Division Engineer. One day he learned that another person would be given the job. He wrote about his reaction to his disappointment:

In a fit of Irish temper and Scotch independence, I marched down to the cable station and sent Priester a hot wire inquiring how come De Kuzmick and not me?

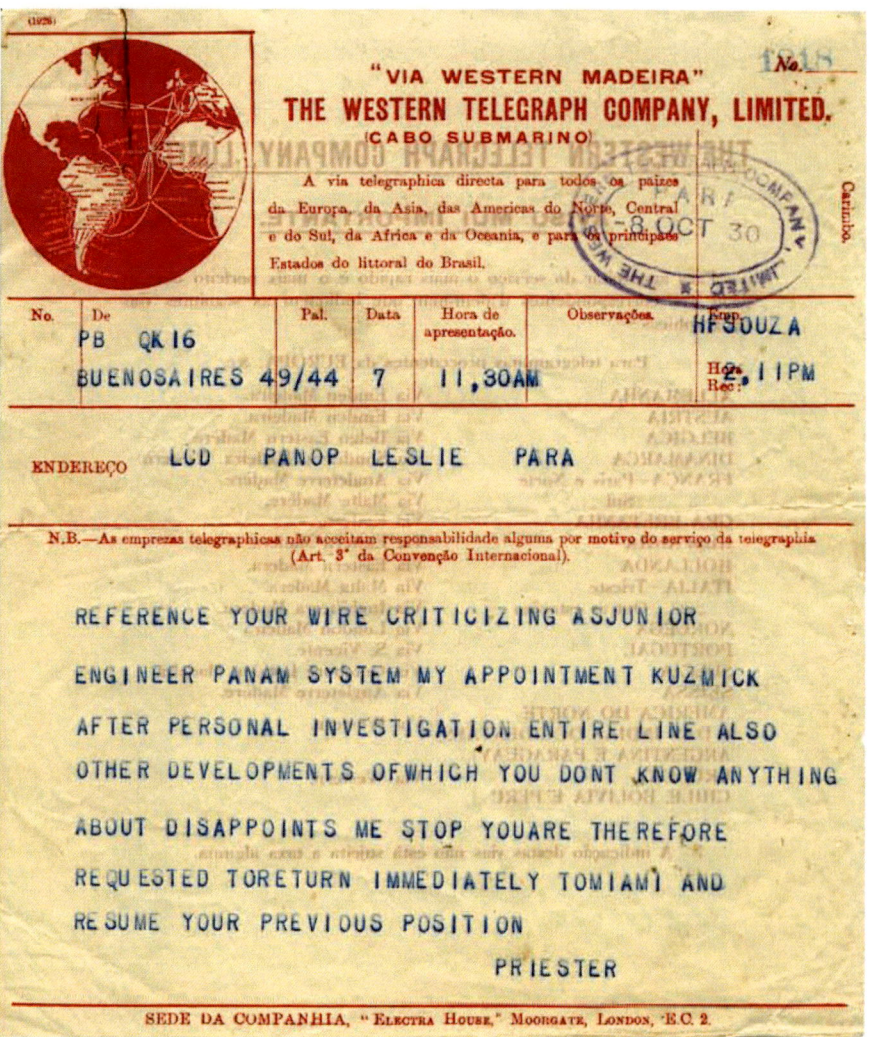

He received this blistering reply and returned to the USA, chastened, and resumed his "previous position."

Leslie's Panair do Brasil lapel pin.

Leslie summarized the experience in his memoirs:

In due course, I was returned to active duty in Miami, and in a spirit of mutual forbearance the company gave me another chance and I gave them one. As so often in life, it was the best thing that could have happened, because I was in the States when the time came to select the Division Engineer for the great job of helping pioneer the TransPacific Service.

His "previous position" was to maintain and prepare for flight the aircraft acquired from NYRBA, mostly Commodores, and a couple of dozen S-38's. In 1931, three brand new Sikorsky S-40s were added to the fleet. These planes were four-engined and could carry 38 passengers, but were primitive compared to the S-42s that Pan Am would use later to pioneer long-range, transoceanic flight.

FIRST SLOAN SCHOLAR AT MIT

In 1931, Alfred P. Sloan, President of General Motors, funded a new program to train talented young engineers early in their careers to administer complex systems and organizations. Leslie was chosen to be one of the first six Sloan Scholars at MIT. It was a stroke of good fortune for all involved. Pan American did not accept Leslie's resignation and instead gave him a leave of absence. In one short year he earned a Master's degree in Engineering and Business Administration.

Just a few years later the skills he learned at MIT were needed in the Pacific and helped determine the difference between success and failure.

When Leslie returned to Miami in 1932 the nation was in the depths of the Great Depression. Unemployment soared to levels never seen, up to 30%. In the previous three years deflation reduced the value of money 22%. Pan American Airways had not returned a penny to its investors and the stock market had crashed. Yet Juan Trippe did not despair. He continued to plan new routes and to order new planes.

A winter day at MIT

Salary Reduction Scales - 1932

Hourly rate of compensation, wage earners	5%
Salaries up to $7,500. per year	10%
Salaries $7,501 to $10,000, inclusive	12.5%
Salaries $10,001 to $12,500, inclusive	15%
Salaries $12,501 to $15,000, inclusive	17.5%
Salaries $15,001 and over	20%

Trippe did, however, ask employees to accept a reduction in their pay to offset the deflation that had greatly reduced the cost of living. In a noble gesture he asked the highest paid to give up the most and the lowest paid to sacrifice only a little.

Trippe concluded his memo to employees, "I am confident that all members of the Pan American Airways System will recognize the equity of this action and will carry on loyally during the current economic depression as they have in the past."

Postcard of a Sikorsky S-40 sent by Leslie's niece.

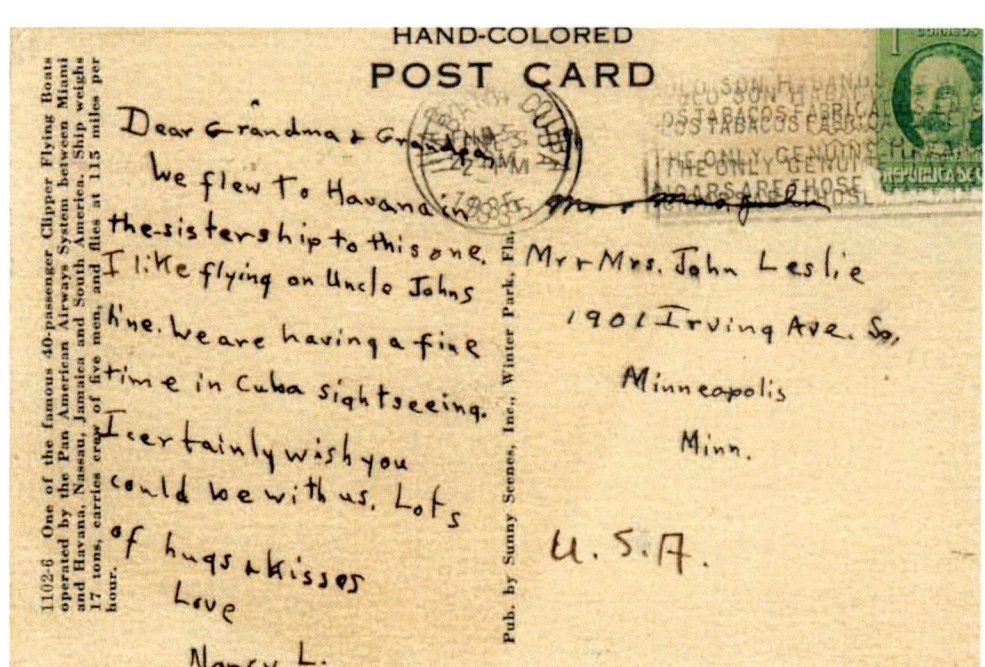

Nancy Leslie sent this postcard from Havana to her grandparents saying, "I like flying on Uncle John's line." She was about 13 years old.

Leslie resumed his "previous position," which had been left open while he attended MIT. By then the Miami and Brownsville, Texas, divisions were flying all over the Caribbean, Central America and both coasts of South America. Their planes were aging and required more maintenance, but their visionary leader, Juan Trippe, was just getting started and soon Pan American would span even longer ocean routes.

A S-40, "The Flying Forest," in the hangar.

This comic strip about Captain Musick is all the more unique because it was written by Captain Eddie Rickenbacker, America's ace fighter pilot of World War I. Rickenbacker would go on to be president of Eastern Airlines. The artist, Clayton Knight, was also an aviator.

The story of Musick building a glider as a boy in 1911 illustrates how close in time aviators of the 1920s were to the first flying machine of 1903. Musick was amazed when his glider crashed, saying, "It looked just like the Wright Bros. plane!"

Leslie's eldest brother, Arnett Leslie of Minneapolis, kept a scrap book of clippings from newspapers about his kid brother's exciting life of pioneering aviation. Clips from this scrapbook appear often in this account of the Pan American Airways career of John Leslie.

CHAPTER 3
"FATHER OF LONG RANGE CRUISING"

Crucial to Trippe's plan was the Sikorsky S-42. Gone was the forest of struts of the S-40; the engines were mounted flush with the wing and were more powerful. With Chief Pilot Ed Musick at the controls Leslie flew hours of test flights to see how the plane could be flown most efficiently—testing, calibrating and calculating and searching for every possible way to increase fuel efficiencies and flight performance.

Sikorsky S-42 Introduced in 1934

Leslie recalled in a speech at Phillips Exeter Academy in 1972:

Some of the tales I share with you relate to our spanning the trackless Pacific with regular airline service. In 1934 I was ordered to go to the headquarters of the Sikorsky Aviation Corporation to confer with the famous airplane designer, Mr. Igor Sikorsky, and his chief engineer, Mr. Mike Gluhareff. We were to discuss long-range, over-ocean flying. These were two of the most eminent aeronautical engineers in the whole world at that time, and I was rather scared at having to sit down with them on ostensibly equal terms to decide how to make one of their aircraft fly much greater distances than ever before.

For two reasons this turned out to be less painful than expected. The first was that Mr. Sikorsky was one of the most courteous, considerate, and modest gentlemen that ever lived. The second was that he and his colleague did not really know much more about long-range flight than I did. Between us, and with the engine and propeller manufacturers, we spent many hours in the air over southern Florida testing out our theories for getting the most miles per gallon out of our flying machines.

Igor Sikorsky and his plant at Bridgeport, CT assembling S-42s and S-43s

Pan Am flying boat Captain Horace Brock cited John Leslie as the "Father of Long Range Cruising" in his book, "Flying the Oceans."

Cruise Control was principally the technique for obtaining the most ground miles per pound of fuel. It was also called Long Range Cruising. It is not the same as Endurance, which is just staying in the air as long as possible. Pounds were used and not gallons and the gallons loaded were converted to pounds because energy was a function of fuel weight and not volume. The pounds were corrected for temperature between 6 lb. and 5 lb. per gallon.

The plane was flown at the angle of attack for maximum L/D (Lift over Drag for the wing section). To maintain this constant angle of attack it was necessary to reduce speed periodically during flight as the gross weight decreased with the consumption of fuel. The father of Long Range Cruising was John C. Leslie who developed it in 1934 and tested it with Musick in the latest S-42 at Miami. This plane was equipped with extra fuel tanks for the Pacific survey flights. Igor Sikorsky, the designer; Gluhareff, the top engineer at the Sikorsky Company; and Tillinghast from Pratt and Whitney, the engine manufacturer, all provided advice.

Leslie's 5 year service pin.

In 1980 author Robert Daley in his book, "AN AMERICAN SAGA Juan Trippe and His Pan Am Empire" described how Leslie and Musick extended the range of the flying boat.

Now forty years old, Musick seemed the same quiet, meticulous man who had flown the first regularly scheduled commercial flight between Havana and Key West seven years before. The general public, which within a year would make Musick the most famous airman in the world after Lindbergh, had never heard of him. It was Musick, together with a young engineer named John Leslie, who did the work from which the technique for long-range cruising crystallized. It was clear that the engines should be turning slowly but laboring hard, like a truck crawling up a steep hill in high gear. But what was this optimum cruising speed, this optimum fuel mixture, this optimum altitude? At what point did a too lean mixture burn out engines? At what point did too much effort cause an engine to explode? Over the Caribbean the tests went on. In the cockpit Leslie stood at Musick's elbow, giving instructions, noting data on his clipboard. There were hours of flying with one engine shut down, with an engine off on either wing, with two engines off on a single wing. Always Leslie and Musick watched the fuel-consumption figures.

Possible emergency procedures were tried out also. A wind-operated pump transferred gas from cabin tanks to wing tanks. Suppose this pump broke down in mid-Pacific? Day after day crewmen practiced pumping the gas out to the wings by hand. There were frequent engine overhauls as well; wear was checked; minor but vital improvements were made.

Leslie described Musick in a **speech to Clipper Pioneers, Rio de Janeiro, in 1975:**

He never seemed to get excited about anything. I myself can see Ed settling down in the cockpit for takeoff, touching, looking, turning, wiggling, somehow as though he had never sat on that particular seat cushion before. He would almost literally draw the cockpit around his shoulders like an old familiar shawl.

I worked most with Ed when we were preparing for the transpacific service. This involved our doing a lot of laborious and not very exciting but very precise flying. The purpose was to measure fuel consumption at various speeds and horsepowers, and at several altitudes. Ed was invariably patient, courteous and cooperative.

After hours of test flights, Leslie prepared the detailed flight program for the famous March 22, 1935, flight that would establish the S-42's range—long enough to fly from San Francisco to Honolulu.

On the next page are part of the cover and an excerpt of that flight program.

Valuable Document
JCL.

Location: Miami
Department: Maintenance
Serial No.: Memorandum
Date: Mar. 22, 1935

JCL
PAA Memorandum

PAN AMERICAN AIRWAYS SYSTEM

REPORT

ON

Suggested Flight Program NC 823M
Non-stop Test Flight, 3/22/35

SUBMITTED

To *Capt. Musick and Capt. Sullivan*

By *J C Leslie*

RECOMMENDED AIR SPEED RANGES
NC-823M, March 22, 1935.
(Reading Air Speed Meters Directly, as Installed and Calibrated March 20, 1935.)

Density Altitude:	1000			3000			5000			12000		
Period	Rec.	Max.	Min.	Rec.	Max.	Min.	Rec.	Max.	Min.	Rec.	Max.	Min.
I	121	126	110	(121)/117	126	110	117	126	110	111.5	126	110
II	117.5	119	107	116.5	119	107	114	119	107	108	119	107
III	113	116	103	112.5	116	103	110	116	103	106	116	103
IV	110	111	100	109	111	100	106	111	100	102	111	100

NOTE: Column headed "Rec." is the recommended indicated air speed for the period and density altitude noted, until further notice. Columns headed "Max." and "Min." indicate the highest and lowest values of indicated air speed which are recommended for long distance flying. The higher values are suggested for lower altitudes and for bumpy air, the lower values being recommended for higher altitudes and smooth air.

The Sikorsky S-42 drew crowds of admirers at the Dinner Key, Miami base. This watercolor by J.W. Golinkin appeared in FORTUNE magazine, April 1936. A Martin M-130 is in the air.

This newspaper clipping appeared about the time of the test flight, but the newspaper and date are unknown.

When the March 22, 1935 flight was completed successfully, the plane was dispatched to San Francisco via Acapulco, Mexico, as there was no water landing facility across the continental USA. Priester cabled Leslie, "DUE TO YOUR INTIMATE KNOWLEDGE S-42," to be in San Francisco for the flying boat's arrival.

This distance is equal to the longest single over-water span across the Pacific from San Francisco to Honolulu. John C. Leslie, Pan American engineer aboard, stated that the trip provided ample basis for estimating the range of the big craft under normal cruising conditions.

Immediately upon her return here the Clipper will be given a complete inspection and servicing in preparation for its trip to San Francisco, by way of Acapulco, Mexico, and San Diego, scheduled for early this week.

John and Jean flew all day and night from Florida to California with their two young children, first "in a little twin engine Curtis," then in "the newest miracle of the time, a Douglas DC-2." It was a grueling flight, but they arrived in time for John to meet the S-42 and to inspect the *SS North Haven*, which would sail the next day laden with all the gear, equipment, provisions and personnel to establish the string of island bases across the Pacific.

```
                    PAN AMERICAN AIRWAYS SYSTEM
                              GENERAL OFFICES
                       CHRYSLER BUILDING, NEW YORK CITY

                                                        MARCH 22, 1935

    MR JOHN C LESLIE
    PAN AMERICAN AIRWAYS INC
    MIAMI FLORIDA


    DUE TO YOUR INTIMATE KNOWLEDGE ESS FORTY TWO FEEL YOU SHOULD BE SAN
    FRANCISCO UPON ARRIVAL NR EIGHT TWENTY THREE M IF POSSIBLE STOP SUGGEST
    YOU AND FAMILY PROCEED MIAMI TO SAN FRANCISCO DOMESTIC AIRLINES POSSIBLY
    ARRANGING ONE OF MECHANICS DRIVE YOUR CAR  PLEASE ADVISE

                                      PRIESTER
```

John Leslie hung Chief Engineer Andre Priester's holiday card on his office wall where it stayed his entire career. The card sums up what is needed for success. The words in the banner are: **THOROUGH, ALERT, RESOURCEFUL, PRUDENT**. The card gives equal weight and importance to operations on the ground and in the air.

"HOW LONG CAN THIS SHIP STAY IN THE AIR?"

PAN AMERICAN AIR WAYS

STAFF HEADS FOR PAN AMERICAN'S PACIFIC DIVISION

| C. M. YOUNG | C. H. SCHILDHAUER | J. C. LESLIE | K. A. KENNEDY |
| Manager, Pacific Division | Division Operations Manager | Acting Division Engineer | Acting Traffic Manager |

Leslie said in the 1972 speech at Phillips Exeter Academy:

Finally, we were ready to transfer our base of operations to San Francisco. This was in the early part of 1935. Our planned route across the Pacific between Honolulu and Manila involved fueling and overnight stops on the islands of Midway, Wake, and Guam. I arrived in San Francisco on the very day that our supply ship was about to leave for these islands. I vividly recall going down to the docks that night and boarding the SS North Haven. *I knew that she had aboard her over a million different items of supplies and equipment, a quarter of a million gallons of gasoline plus 74 construction workers -- everything needed to establish cantonments and operating facilities on these mid-Pacific islands. Midway, about 1,400 miles west northwest from Honolulu, was occupied only by a few men manning a cable relay station. Wake, some, 1,300 miles west of Midway, had never been settled by anyone. Guam was easier, of course, because the United States had gotten it from Spain in the Spanish-American War (1898) and it had long been a US Navy base.*

Looking up at the steep, black sides of that vessel in the foggy San Francisco night and realizing the indispensable part that it had to play in our forthcoming adventure, gave me a feeling of awe and a shiver of anticipation. I could talk for an hour, of course, concerning our adventures in constructing these island bases. I would just say that our lack of modern heavy equipment and tools, as compared to those used just a few years later for overseas base construction during World War II, was spectacular. I just don't see how our men did it.

Leslie remembers the first flight in his memoirs. He knew the risks they were taking, challenging the boundaries of technology and the skill of the flight crew.

Soon we were ready to undertake the first leg of our survey flights — that is, from San Francisco to Honolulu. At 3:50 p.m. on April 16, 1935, the Sikorsky flying boat, license NR 823 M, taxied out on San Francisco Bay and pointed her nose toward the west. It was late in the afternoon on a cool, clear, sunny, sparkling day with a fresh breeze and a moderate sea. The aircraft was overloaded, but we knew it had the power to pull itself off the water. As Division Engineer, responsible for the mechanical condition of the aircraft and for the range computations, I was in the patrol launch alongside the takeoff. When Captain Eddie Musick 'gave her the gun,' I remember thinking to myself, 'Here goes everything or nothing.' Had we failed, it would have been an enormous setback for over-ocean flying and US flag aviation. The flight to Honolulu was uneventful and consumed almost precisely the amount of fuel that we had forecast.

The Sikorsky S-42 departs the Golden Gate Bridge and arrives at Diamond Head.

NEW YORK Herald

(Copyright, 1935, New York Tribune Inc.)

THURSDAY, APRIL 18, 1935

THE MINNEAPOLIS JOURNAL April 19, 1935

HAWAII, HO! AND RECORD, TOO!

Clipper Flies To Honolulu In 17¾ Hours

Establishes First Leg of Trans-Pacific Service by Record Jump on Exact Scheduled Time

Carried Crew of 6 And Mail 'Payload'

'Had no Difficulty,' Says Capt. Musick, Arriving With Unfatigued Aids

The return trip four days later, however, nearly proved the skeptics right. The Clipper encountered strong head winds and was unable to determine its position due to cloud cover. It could not even determine drift during a large portion of the trip. The radio direction finder was providing information on their position, but it only told them they were headed to San Francisco, not how close they were. Finally they got a celestial fix and knew just where they were, a long way from home!

Station crew and aircrew wives waited with growing anxiety as the minutes ticked by. "How long can this ship stay aloft?" one asked. "Maybe twenty four hours," somebody said, optimistically. After 21 hours in the air the Clipper hove into view and alighted on the waters of San Francisco Bay, 3 1/4 hours longer than the trip outbound. Everyone gave a sigh of relief. The flight engineer checked the fuel tanks with a dip stick. It was just barely damp at the bottom, a close call.

Praise and congratulations came in from outside and inside the company.

Letter from A.W. Marshall who worked on the engines with Leslie

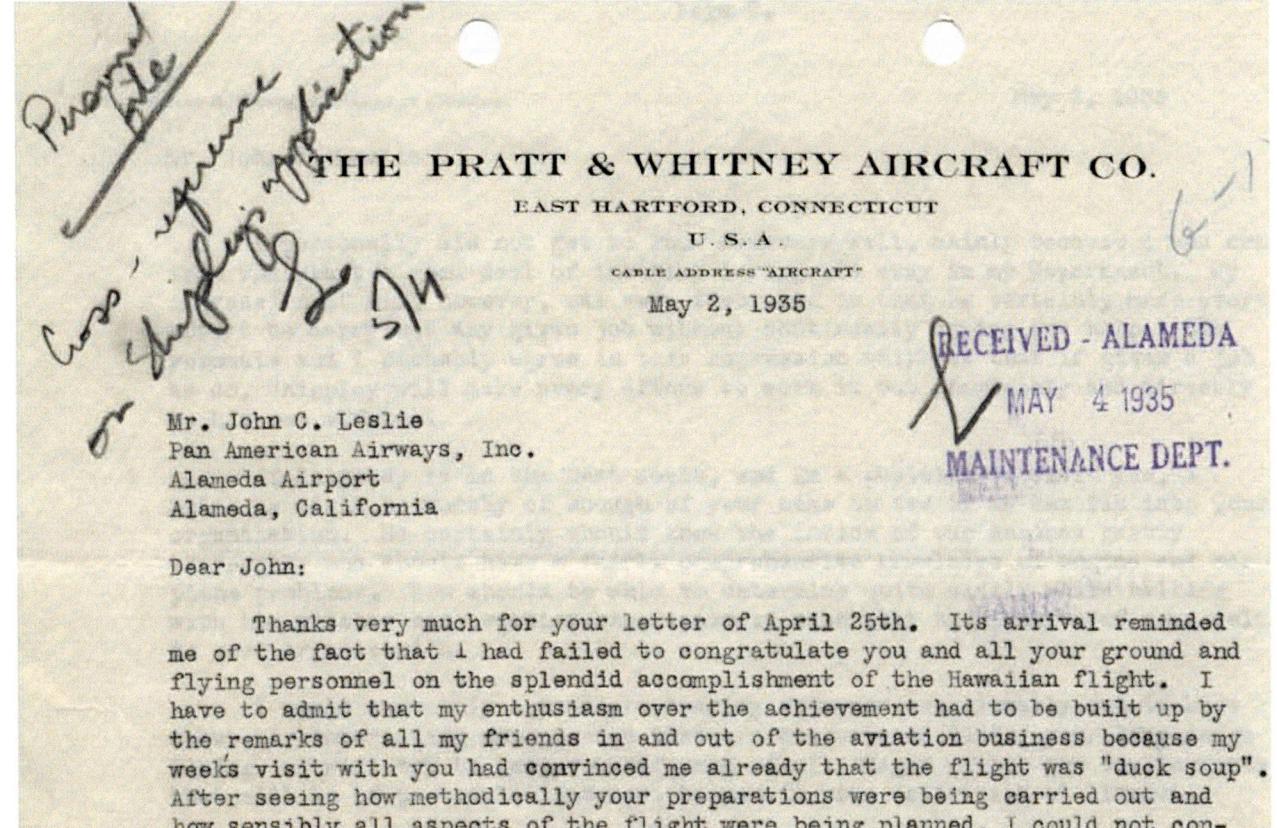

PAN AMERICAN AIRWAYS, INC.

GENERAL OFFICES - CHRYSLER BUILDING - NEW YORK CITY

MIAMI OFFICE - P. O. BOX 3311, MIAMI, FLORIDA

Personal
John J.S.

Miami, Florida
May 8, 1935

Mr. John C. Leslie
Pan American Airways, Inc.
Alameda Airport
Alameda, California

Dear John:

Everybody here was overjoyed at the successful flights to and from Honolulu and although it is true that the Caribbean Division did a lot of work preparing the plane, we nevertheless realize that you were right here on the spot when this work was going on and that if any credit is to be heaped on somebody's head, we are unable to single out anybody else but you to get it.

I still think that you should take a drive down through the forest of giant sequoias some fine clear day with Mrs. Leslie and compose yourself in the shade of those trees to be at one with the Universe again.

Your old friend, Captain Terletzky, just now heaves on the scene and so I will stop writing to you, at the same time expressing our mutual regard.

Sincerely,

H. W. Toomey

PAN AMERICAN AIRWAYS, INC.

GENERAL OFFICES - CHRYSLER BUILDING - NEW YORK CITY

April 18, 1935.

PERSONAL

Mr. John C. Leslie,
Pan American Airways, Inc.,
Alameda Airport,
Alameda, California.

Dear Mr. Leslie:

    The development of the S-42 for ocean flights and the great mass of detail which was necessary in preparation for these flights has culminated in the successful completion of the first long distance commercial flight. It is evident from the smoothness and efficiency with which this flight was carried out that your organization is already functioning according to the traditional standards of the Pan American Airways regardless of the fact that it is in itself an entirely new unit of the System. The responsibility of the maintenance and servicing of equipment is undoubtedly one of the most important factors for the successful commercial operation of aircraft and you have every reason to be proud of these first successful results of your young organization. The smoothness of the entire project is adequate testimony to the effect that the experience and policies of the Company are being carefully applied in your organization and I have every confidence that the highest standards of the System will at all times be maintained in the Pacific Division.

    With kindest regards.

Yours very truly,

A. A. Priester.

THE JOHN LESLIE PAPER CO.
301 SOUTH FIFTH STREET
MINNEAPOLIS, MINNESOTA

April 11, 1935

Dear Jean:

When this letter reaches you history will have been made in trans-Pacific air transportation, and John will have taken an important part in this epoch-making event.

This letter has traveled by air from Minneapolis to San Francisco (via regular U. S. air mail), hence by Pan-American Pioneer Clipper ship, S-42, to Hawaii, there deposited in U. S. mail for transport by water to San Francisco and by air San Francisco to Alameda.

Yours in the cause of Philatelic history,

Arnett

Mrs. John C. Leslie
℅ Pan-American Airways
Alameda Airport
Alameda, Calif.

The Air Route Across the Pacific, Over Which Regular Flights Are Expected to Begin This Summer.

THE MINNEAPOLIS TRIBUNE: SUNDAY JUNE 16 1935

Pan American Clipper Lands at Midway Isle

By Associated Press.

Alameda, Calif., June 15.—The Pan American Clipper plane alighted at Midway island at 8:40 p. m., eastern standard time, completing its 1,323 mile flight from Pearl Harbor, Hawaii.

The overseas journey to the mid-Pacific island was completed in nine hours and 13 minutes of flying time.

The flight marked the first commercial air venture west of Hawaii.

From the scrap book of Arnett Leslie, Minneapolis.

After the first flight to Honolulu the S-42 continued on survey flights to Midway, then Wake, and finally to Guam.

Regular service was gradually introduced between San Francisco and Honolulu, first for mail, then for passengers.

Clipper Ship Makes Hop to Midway Isle

Flying Boat Covers 1,388 Miles in 9 Hours, 13 Minutes

Tiny Dots in Pacific

TAKING DELIVERY OF THE *CHINA CLIPPER*

In October of 1935, Pacific Division Engineer John Leslie, the delivery team, Chief Pilot Ed Musick and a flight crew went to Baltimore to take delivery of the Martin M-130, named the *China Clipper*. The delivery of America's longest range, most modern airplane was amply covered by the press, especially when Charles Lindbergh took the plane for a test flight. After the celebrations they took the new flying boat to Miami for extensive testing and from there to California for the inaugural Pacific flight. Leslie and Musick were interviewed in the air by NBC.

John Leslie was responsible for maintenance of the aircraft, preparing it for flight and establishing the flight plan. He was as proud of holding Civil Aeronautics Authority certificates as Aircraft and Aircraft Engine Mechanic as he was of his two degrees from MIT. He was also a certified Aircraft Dispatcher.

The photo shows him in coveralls climbing over the China Clipper on its delivery flight.

Veteran pilot Marius Lodeesen, wrote about first meeting Leslie. English was not his native language so it is evident he meant "disassembling."

And I remember a blond young man in white coveralls dissembling a Wasp engine in the overhaul shop at 36th Street, who came to me held out his hand and said: "I am John Leslie."

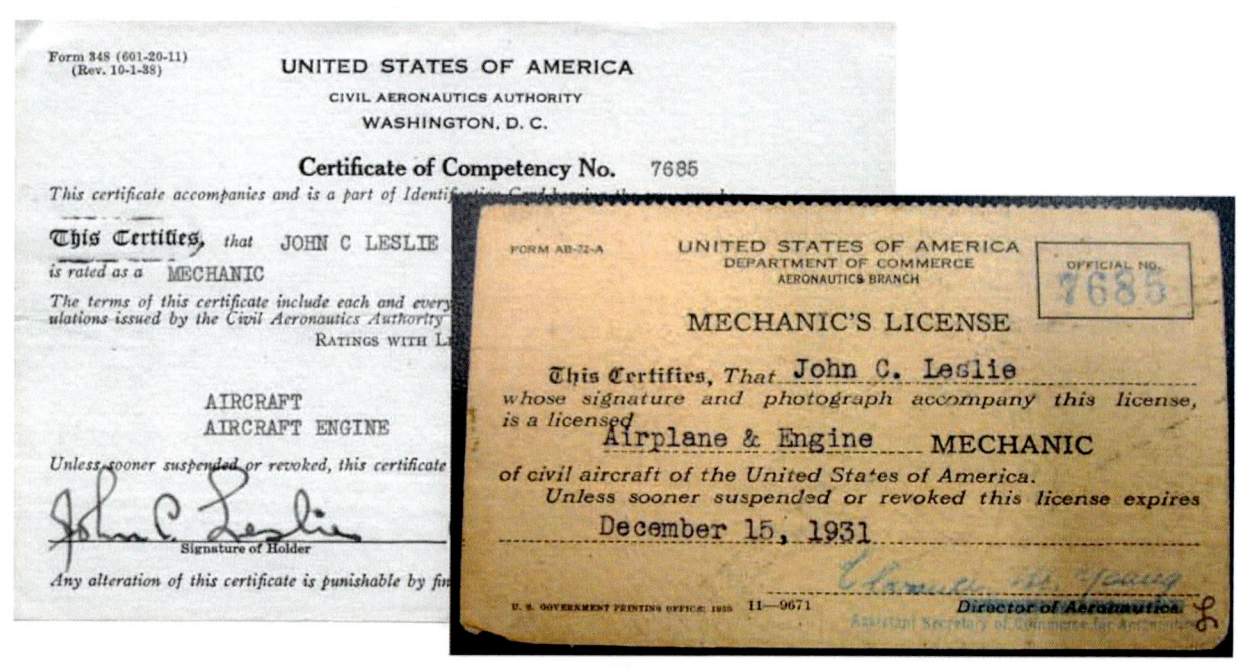

CHINA CLIPPER WAITING TEST FLIGHTS HERE

America's Largest Airplane Arrives on Hop From Baltimore

CHINA CLIPPER TO HOP FOR WEST TOMORROW

Nonstop Flight To Acapuco On Mexican Coast Is the First Leg

nov 7 1935

The China Clipper arrived here from Baltimore October 27. The transpacific service is scheduled to start November 22 from San Francisco. John Leslie, Pacific division engineer, was in charge of flights in Miami.

The *China Clipper* passed all her final test flights in Miami with flying colors and left for California via Acapulco with Leslie and the delivery team aboard.

This watercolor by J.W. Golinkin, appeared in FORTUNE magazine, April, 1936. It depicts the China Clipper tied up at Pan American's Dinner Key Terminal in Miami.

CHAPTER 4
"I THRILL TO THE WONDER OF IT ALL"

"The heartfelt congratulations of an air-minded sailor: I thrill to the wonder of it all." — Franklin Delano Roosevelt, President of the United States, November 22, 1935.

The successful flights of the *China Clipper* from San Francisco to Manila, via the island bases, captured the imagination of Americans and people around the world. It was headline news comparable to the landing on the moon in 1969 and the space shuttle launch in 1981. Captain Musick became a national figure, although he did not much enjoy it. His description to the press of a good flight was often just, "Uneventful," or "Without incident." Leslie was content, as usual, to remain behind the scenes. In the only photo of him with the flying boat on that famous day you can see the edge of his signature derby hat, just like the one worn by his father. Leslie even recalls going to his job interview with Andre Priester, "...proudly wearing, believe it or not, a derby hat!"

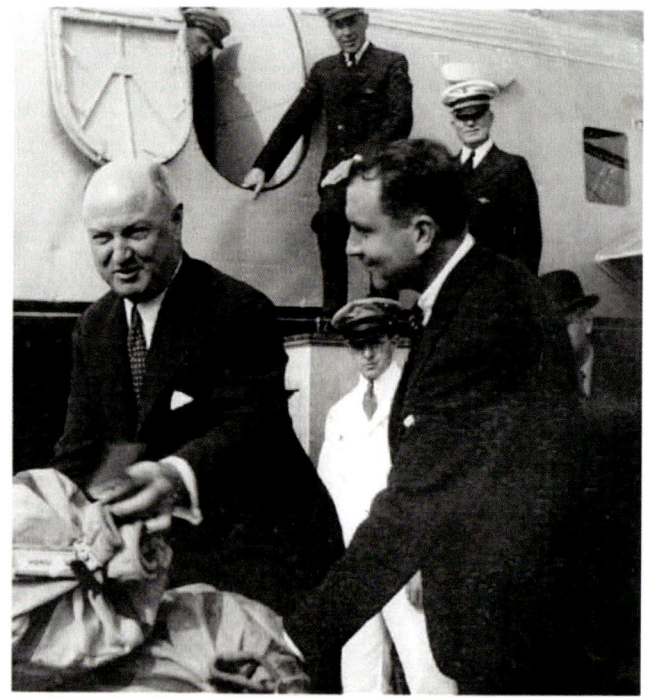

Postmaster General Farley delivers the first TransPacific airmail to Juan Trippe. Leslie's derby is seen behind Trippe's shoulder.

Jean Leslie was sitting in the grandstand second row on the right, shown in this New York Times Magazine Section cover photo. Jean often proudly recalled the historic event, one that justified her husband's hard work and long hours.

Thousands of Californians were given time off to crowd the shoreline to watch and cheer the world's largest, longest-range aircraft undertake the momentous feat. In the depths of the Great Depression the flight became a ray of hope symbolizing that by hard work, daring and inspiration America could lift itself out of the economic morass. School children were let out of school and those still alive 75 years later remember the excitement.

In Minneapolis John's parents listened to the radio intently as the departure ceremonies were broadcast across the nation.

They sent this cable to their son. One can only imagine the depth of their pride and wonder.

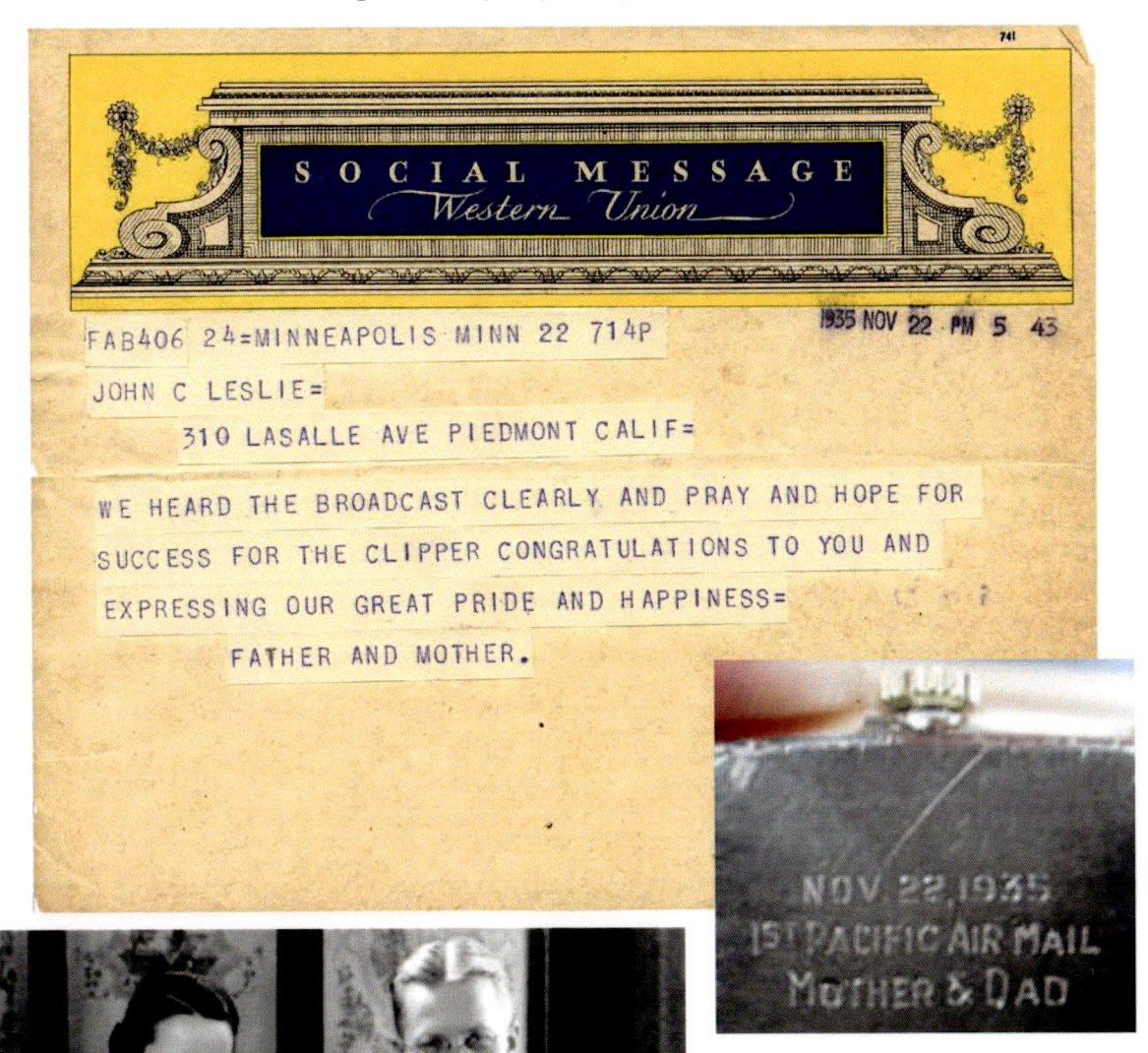

SOCIAL MESSAGE
Western Union

FAB406 24=MINNEAPOLIS MINN 22 714P   1935 NOV 22 PM 5 43

JOHN C LESLIE=
    310 LASALLE AVE PIEDMONT CALIF=

WE HEARD THE BROADCAST CLEARLY AND PRAY AND HOPE FOR SUCCESS FOR THE CLIPPER CONGRATULATIONS TO YOU AND EXPRESSING OUR GREAT PRIDE AND HAPPINESS=
    FATHER AND MOTHER.

NOV 22, 1935
1st PACIFIC AIR MAIL
MOTHER & DAD

To commemorate the accomplishment they also sent him this gold watch engraved:

NOV. 22, 1935
1st PACIFIC AIR MAIL
MOTHER & DAD

It still keeps good time.

Jean and John with Polly and John

PAN AMERICAN AIRWAYS, INC.

GENERAL OFFICES - CHRYSLER BUILDING - NEW YORK CITY

OFFICE OF THE PRESIDENT

November 22 1935

Mr. John C. Leslie,
Division Engineer, Pacific Division
Pan American Airways, Inc.
Alameda Airport
Alameda, California

Dear John:

    This letter will have been transported by the Pan American Airways System on the first scheduled air service to operate over a major ocean route -- that between the United States and the Philippines. I hope it will serve as a permanent record of this new milestone in transportation as well as of your personal contribution to this pioneer undertaking.

    May I, on my own behalf and on behalf of our Board of Directors, express my appreciation of your loyal teamwork and cooperation during the past years of preparatory work. I am confident that without your assistance it could not have been successfully inaugurated.

Sincerely,

J. T. Trippe
President

J. T. Trippe
PAN AMERICAN AIRWAYS SYSTEM
427 POST STREET
SAN FRANCISCO, CALIFORNIA

S.F.-P.I.

VIA AIR MAIL

Mr. J. C. Leslie
310 La Salle Street
Piedmont, California

SAN FRANCISCO, CALIF. NOV 22 1 PM 1935

The *China Clipper* flew for five days at an average flight time of 12 hours per day. It stopped overnight at Honolulu, Midway, Wake, Guam and then alighted in Manila after 59 hours of flight. This was considered a marvel that shortened the time for travel between the two distant points on the globe from a month to a few days

TIME magazine, December 2, 1935, put Captain Musick's photo on its cover

The China Clipper passed the Golden Gate Bridge and headed west over the vast Pacific Ocean. The crowd watched as it became just a silver speck and then disappeared over the horizon. They had seen history being made.

Leslie wrote in his 1975 manuscript for the Pan Am History Project:

Captain Musick's take-off from San Francisco Bay with the China Clipper was slightly spectacular and is claimed by the author (Leslie) to have been the partial cause for his prematurely white hair at the age of 30. In any event, Musick got off in nice order but, with the engine cowl flaps open, saw that he was not climbing rapidly enough to pass over the Oakland Bay Bridge, then under construction, but cables, ropes and scaffolding were still hanging down below it. Musick calmly decided to fly under it and, in the words of Victor Wright, the Flight Engineer, 'We all ducked.'

There were several small airplanes taking pictures of the take-off for the newspapers and they resolutely followed him under the bridge. At this low altitude, Musick was able to fly the China Clipper *past the thousands and thousands of school children lined up along the Marina and then climb enough to pass over the cables of the new Golden Gate Bridge, which were just being strung at that time. Old timers will exclaim 'Oh, I remember.'*

The reception of the China Clipper *at Manila is said to have been a high water mark for the size and enthusiasm of the crowd. Vice President Bixby of Pan American was there and never forgot the unbelievably emotional outburst of the Philippine people. If memory serves right, the crowds even tried to carry the automobile in which Captain Musick was sitting bodily up the street.*

"MAKE MEN AND MACHINES WORK TOGETHER"

After the successful crossing of the *China Clipper*, weekly flights began. At first they only carried the mail, but passengers followed in late 1936. Technical difficulties arose at a steady rate, but were solved with the assistance of the aircraft, engine and propeller manufacturers. The planes themselves needed constant maintenance and, as there were only three Martin M-130's and a few S-42's in the Pacific, the demands on human and mechanical resources were heavy. In addition, the island bases required steady support of all kinds. Leslie's files indicate a sense of near desperation.

Leslie wrote of these challenges, the first to an old friend, and the second to his boss.

The past year and a half have been intensely interesting, and equally busy. The first 9 or 10 months were a madhouse, with work going on 7 days a week and all hours of the day and night. As an example, I brought about 15 maintenance people out here from Miami and Brownsville and now have something over 200 in my department. That has taken a great deal of training and organization, as you will well be able to imagine.

My aeronautical engineering has had to spread itself very thinly over a most amazing field of things having to do with the operation and maintenance of small villages, such as fresh water supply, refrigerators, Diesel electric power plants, and all the rest. As a matter of fact, the fascinating thing about this work is that it not only involves all kinds of engineering, but a substantial amount of personnel and financial management.

I am quite naturally enthusiastic about the commercial possibilities for air transport in the Pacific. I think our President and Board of Directors displayed an amazing amount of courage and vision in undertaking the project, and I am firmly convinced that they will be repaid in future years.

-3-

Excerpt from Leslie's letter to Col. Young, Pacific Division Manager.   April 16, 1936

8. We have several times discussed the problem of flying the routes laid out for us, at the frequencies indicated, with only three ships. I must note again that if it can be done at all, it can be done only for a relatively brief period of months. I presume that you will investigate the attitude of our people in New York to this general question, not only in the Chief Engineer's office, but elsewhere, and that you will dispell undue optimism that you may encounter. Also, that you will ascertain what steps are being taken to supply us with adequate flying equipment.

As a natural concomitant of the above, I presume that you will ascertain what plans there are for flying from Manila to the China Coast, and whether they will involve basing an airplane at Manila.

9. And as a natural result of all of the above, I must note here my thought that it will be a matter of many months before we shall be properly able to handle a passenger service. From the standpoint of flying equipment alone, our present machines have not demonstrated the necessary degree of reliability.

Passenger service started toward the end of 1936 and the island bases were improved constantly so that passengers disembarking for the night would have decent accommodations. It was a prodigious feat to supply and maintain these facilities and Leslie faced the constant challenge of ensuring that maintenance would be performed at the highest level.

Ian Marshall, artist and aviation historian, described Leslie as a man "who could make men and machines work together." Leslie's papers show a deep concern for the human side of enterprise. Just one example: he wrote a memo to encourage the employees to view ALL parts of an aircraft as equally important. His colleagues in the other divisions wrote to him saying that they were going to give talks and write memos along the same lines—the sincerest form of flattery.

Excerpt from the memo to employees.

```
(To be posted on bulletin boards, Alameda.          cc:  Division Manager
 Sent to islands & Chief Mechanics).                      Chief Engineer

        All Employees
        Maintenance
        Alameda
                                                          Division Engineer
                                                          Maintenance
                                                          Alameda
```

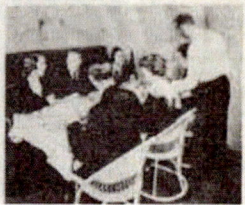

This memorandum is addressed primarily to those members of our organization industry who are relatively new in the aviation industry. While I offer it only as a personal opinion, I have checked my thoughts with some other people who have had mature experience in the industry and find a substantial agreement.

I think I have noticed a tendency upon the part of some of our younger people to be governed by superstitions and ideas that cannot possibly be conducive to their ultimate future progress.

First, there is a kind of superstition that the engine is the most wonderful and the most important part of an airplane and consequently that anybody who works on an engine becomes a member of some sort of aristocracy. Almost every High School boy asking for his first job indicates a kind of longing to work "on the engines". When he gets a chance to work on the engines he feels himself to be some kind of superior being. I assure you that nothing could be further from the case. Of course the engines are important, but **not** a bit more important than innumerable other parts of the airplane. Suppose that you personally were flying from Alameda to Honolulu. Which would you rather have happen, one engine fail or the main elevator control cable fail? One engine fail or all of your instruments go out of commission? And so on indefinitely. In short, every single job that is done on one of our airplanes is important and there cannot possibly be any particular glory or prestige attached to any one job.

Another example of Leslie's concern for morale and efficiency is this memo about communications. In it he addresses a 1930s problem of communicating mostly in writing and with long delays in the mail. It seems almost quaint by 21st century standards that John Leslie takes some comfort in having seen most of his crew within the last twelve months.

PAN AMERICAN AIRWAYS SYSTEM

Memorandum

August 3, 1937.

Chief Mechanics　　　　　　　　　　　　　　　　Division Engineer

Maintenance　　　　　　　　　　　　　　　　　　Maintenance

Honolulu, Midway, Wake, Guam, Manila,　　　　　Alameda
　　Macau and Hongkong

Organization　　　　　　　PERSONAL

I am going to write the following just as it comes to mind, in a very informal manner. Please read it as though we could all be talking together.

In any organization like ours, there is the inherent problem of trying to get things done when the people doing them are a long ways apart. Most of the time there is no way to do this except written communication, although personal visits are certainly useful and we try to arrange them as often as time and money permit.

Written communication is not a very satisfactory means of getting things done, when it is not accompanied by frequent personal contact. Furthermore, the longer you use writing to convey ideas between people who never see each other, the more unsatisfactory the thing becomes. To a certain extent, the method "carries with it the seed of its own destruction". Therefore, we must try to see each other as often as possible. You may find it hard to believe, but I have several times tried to make an inspection trip and each time circumstances have intervened. I have been somewhat comforted by the fact that most of you have been in Alameda within the past 12 months.

The manufacturers of equipment also believed personal contact was important as illustrated by John Leslie recalling in a letter to a friend escorting Igor Sikorsky to Pan Am's seaplane base in San Francisco Bay:

Did you ever hear the story of our great airplane designer, Igor Sikorsky, looking over the stern of a San Francisco ferryboat at the (begging) gulls?

He watched them intently for quite a long time, and then he exclaimed, 'If those birds only knew how to fly!'

Subject: Itinerary - John C. Leslie

Leslie went "out on the line" regularly and his files contain various trips such as the this one in 1937.

For the information of those concerned, my itinerary during my absence from Alameda commencing September 8 is as follows:

U. S. date throughout

```
Lv.  Alameda........September 8............Trip 143
Arr. Honolulu......."         9
"    Midway........."        10
"    Wake..........."        11                      ....(One week layover)
Lv.  Wake..........."        19............Trip 145
Arr. Guam..........."        20
"    Manila........."        21
"    Hong Kong....."         22
"    Manila........."        23............Trip 146
"    Guam..........."        24
"    Wake..........."        25
"    Midway........."        26
"    Honolulu......."        27                      ....(One week layover)
Lv.  Honolulu......October   4............Trip 148
Arr. Alameda........"         5
```

Serious problems had to be solved, such as this one from Leslie's memoirs:

The aircraft was powered with the Pratt Whitney Twin Wasp engine, which later became very well known as the acme of reliability. However, the Twin Wasp model "A" was plagued with a difficulty of a most radical sort in its master rod bearing. This is the main bearing in a radial engine that is the connection between the pistons and the crankshaft. Something had gone wrong with the design or selection of materials for this bearing with the result that, very shortly after installing a newly overhauled engine, the master rod bearing would completely fail. I personally saw several of the Martin M-130 aircraft venture out on San Francisco Bay for test flights only to return within 15 or 20 minutes with another master rod bearing burned out.

As Division Engineer, I had direct responsibility for this condition and we were all beside ourselves, not only with the problem of getting the aircraft ready for transpacific flight, but also with doing so safely. Obviously, we could not send aircraft out over the Pacific with main bearings that might fail.

In accordance with the fine Yankee tradition of the Pratt Whitney Aircraft Company in Hartford, Connecticut, the builders of the engine, worked night and day for a solution. Fortunately, such a solution was found in the form of a softer bearing, as I recall. Someone had thought it would be an improvement to install a harder bearing with large silver content, but this was wrong, so they fell back on their older types of bearing construction. Mechanical epidemics of this kind are naturally unsettling to the captains and flight crews but I think I hardly realized it at the time. Because we were all one solid team with a common endeavor we shared all of our troubles whether aloft or ashore. At no time do I recollect any expressed feeling of alarm or opposition on the part of the flight crews.

Sometimes the island bases had strange requests. Imagine the puzzlement at the San Francisco headquarters over a requisition for "Irish Moss" for use on a mid-Pacific island! Or, a plowshare for Midway where one could only plow sand and rock!

While out at the island bases, sometimes with long layovers, Leslie found more than enough time to compile extensive lists of things-to-do such as just this one page of nine shown below.

> One day one of the island bases demanded several square yards of Irish moss.
>
> **ODD REQUEST**
>
> That had maintenance down for a while. Mr. Leslie and his aides discovered in an old cook book that Irish moss is used in some recipes. However, a more logical explanation was that the stuff was wanted to plant on the sandy wastes of the island.
>
> So maintenance obligingly obtained the specified number of yards of Irish moss and shipped it out on the next plane. And how the island sputtered! What was really wanted was Irish felt to line the hull of its motorboat.
>
> But a request from Midway capped the climax. Midway wanted—of all things—a plowshare.
>
> "Can you imagine that—in the aviation business?" Mr. Leslie chuckles. "Why, I don't think I ever saw a plowshare before."

AIRCRAFT

1. Positive means of keeping passengers out of crew's quarters.
2. Reduce weight of equipment and furnishings. Example - coat hangers, drift bomb racks, paper towel holders, trays, tables, etc.
   Assign apprentice engineer.
3. Test periscope type drift sight through hull at Navigator's table.
4. Safety cord on Kollsman drift sight to prevent loss.
5. Change interior furnishings:
   a. Install tables for serving meals with table covers having elastic bands on corners to hold on table.
   b. Install table or other furniture in lounge to break up monotonous appearance.
   c. Revise water heater to provide heat for food.
   d. Coat rack for crew forward in pilot's compartment.
   e. Map in lounge with moveable airplane to show position every two or three hours.
6. Provide protection for side of ship from baggage stowed in sleeping compartment.
7. Supply Kollsman drift sight with light for night use - same as octant.
8. Safety of cabin lights in gas vapors.
9. Study heat and ventilation as ranges appear inadequate. Heat particularly bad in upper berths - almost unbearable.
10. Move radio transmitter forward, antenna from wing strut, to facilitate and reduce radio work.

No picture of island base life is complete without the nestling 'Gooney birds' (Laysan Albatross) and Pan American's million-mile pilot, Captain Ed Musick, on Wake Island.

A long memo from Leslie to Col. Young from Wake starts with the salutary effects of island living, and goes on to the myriad details of running an island base.

```
Division Manager                              Nov 7 1940
Asst. Operations Manager ✓                    Operations Manager

Exec - Opns                                   Operations

Treasure Island                               Now & Wake


Wake - General - Confidential


Dear Colonel and Thurston:

This is just a note to say hello and confirm some of the notes I have sent you
by radio. Needless to say, I have chafing a bit under these schedule delays,
knowing how much grief they must have been causing you in Sfc - also wishing
that I might have been able to spread the same amount of time over more
airports. But so it goes in this strange business of ours -- if it can be
called a business. Of course, my time on Wake has been far from wasted. There
has been lots to do and I have found the physical exercise and fresh air most
welcome; I only wish I could find its counterpart in Sfc! Also, it is very
valuable every couple of years to get into the spirit of this very unique
island life. Finally, I think I know almost every nook and cranny within
our compound, and I have tramped over godly portions of the island group as
well.
```

"TO OUR UTTER SADNESS"

It might be an exaggeration to say that John Leslie saw it coming, but from this excerpt from a memo to Ed McVitty in the Chief Engineer's office in New York, it is certain he knew the risks were great and foreshadowed the loss of the *Samoan Clipper* in January, 1938

> As another example, we had a recent trip on which the captain had made one trip in independent command prior to this one, the first officer had made only three trips, and the other members of the flight crew had made only one or two Manila round trips. You will readily see that the safety factor in such a case is about as low as one can put up with in an operation of this kind.
>
> Now we have facing us the New Zealand operation, with such severe limitations upon personnel, flying equipment, and airport characteristics that it is going to take the utmost experience and discrimination to avoid a hazardous operation.

From Leslie's memoirs:

... the choice of Pago Pago Harbor for the first flights to New Zealand was marginal at best. The airplane had to approach over a considerable range of hills, make a steep descent to the water and get down before it got to the other end of the harbor where the ocean swells were quite large. For taking off they had to start way up at the end of the inshore end of the harbor and hope they got off the water before encountering the same swells. On his second trip to New Zealand, Musick's take-off was ordinary and he was an hour en route when he radioed that he had an oil leak and he was turning back to Pago Pago. One does not know, of course, whether the oil leak was minor or major or whether in the event it would have been better to have continued in level flight to New Zealand. In any event, Musick elected to return. In order to land at all, much less under these adverse conditions, the aircraft had to be lightened by dumping gasoline. This was done at that time by releasing the valves in the bottom of the wing tanks. When the dump valves were opened the aircraft caught fire and plunged to its destruction.

Leslie went on to say:

While this method of dumping gasoline was standard at the time, and I personally had been in aircraft running dump valve tests, it had never occurred to any of us that a fire hazard existed. The fact was, however, that there was no chute out into the air stream from the dump valve hole and therefore some of the gasoline wetted the lower surface of the wing in the area where there was stagnant air due to the boundary layer. Something ignited the gasoline vapor in the air behind the aircraft and the flame propagated upstream until it ignited the gasoline on the lower surface of the wing, with catastrophic results.

This immediately prompted an urgent redesign of all the fuel dumping facilities on all American transport aircraft. Such is the price of ignorance or progress! I only wish we had been as successful in the end result as were the crew of Apollo 13 who had the bad explosion aboard their spaceship and limped back home safely but under very perilous conditions.

Here's Pan American Account of Tragedy

J. T. Trippe, president and general manager of Pan-American Airways, gave the Associated Press the following account of the Samoan Clipper's tragic flight today:

"About one hour out, Captain Edwin C. Musick reported an oil leak on his No. 4 motor and that he was turning back to Pago Pago.

"At 8:27, local time, approximately two hours after his departure from Pago Pago, Captain Musick radioed to the Pan-American Airways station at Pago Pago that he expected to land at that point in about ten minutes and was signing off preparatory to dumping sufficient gas to trim the ship to proper landing weight.

"No further word was received from the ship."

Trippe said he believed Captain Musick and his flight crew are entirely blameless.

"Radio reports from the plane prove that on this flight, as on all previous flights, he carefully followed the most conservative operating technique possible," Trippe asserted.

"Needless to say, everyone connected with Pan American Airways is grieved beyond expression at the untimely fate of Captain Musick and his splendid crew.

"At this time, with all details yet unknown, we can only express the belief that after a thorough analysis of the possible causes of the fire, a way will be found to prevent a re-occurrence.

"The death of Captain Musick and his crew is an irreparable blow to our company and will be a distinct loss to American aviation.

"Captain Musick contributed much to American prestige in the air."

Ian Marshall's watercolor shows the S-42 at Pago Pago and challenges of the steep hills of the approach and of alighting in the small harbor.

The loss of America's most famous pilot after Charles Lindbergh was headline news throughout the nation and the world.

Clipper Missing In South Pacific; Musick, 6 Aboard

Oil Slick on Ocean Stirs Fear Huge Plane May Be Wrecked

PILOT'S WIFE CALM

Mrs. Musick 'Sure' He's Safe

Mrs. Edwin C. Musick
Friends Keep Vigil With Her.

Daring Sky Skipper's Mate Confident Musick Will Come Through

Sadly, Cleo Musick's optimism and hope did not bring her husband and his crew back. She was so distraught at the memorial service she collapsed.

The San Francisco Bay community turned out in force out to honor its fallen heroes.

Throng Mourns at S. F. Services for Heroes of Clipper

South Sea Crash Victims Honored by Impressive City Hall Rites

Simplicity, sincerity, dignity—these qualities yesterday marked San Francisco's public tribute to the lost heroes of the Samoan Clipper...

San Francisco Examiner

TUESDAY — PART TWO — SAN FRANCISCO, JANUARY 25, 1938 — TUESDAY

City's Tribute to Pathfinders of Air

THEIR MEMORY SHALL ★★★ LIVE ON FOREVER

> Rabbi Rudolph I. Coffee spoke the invocation. City Attorney John J. O'Toole, chairman of the occasion, expressed the city's sense of loss. Then John Leslie, no orator but just a fellow-flying man, said in simple words what his co-workers thought of the seven men of the Samoan Clipper. Leslie is assistant division manager for Pan-American Airways here.

Leslie gave the eulogy on behalf of Pan American:

Mayor Rossi - Friends:

I should like to think that we are here today, not as officials and citizens of a city, not as members of a business organization, but only as friends, gathered to honor the memory of friends. To most of us, Captain Musick, Captain Sellers, Frederick MacLean, John Brooks, John Stickrod, Paul Brunk, and Thomas Findley were not names in headlines, not anonymous officers of an American airplane, but were 'Ed' and 'Pop' and 'Jack,' companions in the work of the world. So it is that their personalities and their characters live in our thoughts today.

A century ago, the officers and men of our merchant marine carried the American flag over new seas and into strange ports, until it was recognized the world over as a symbol of expert, courageous seamanship. Some of those ships never returned from their voyages. So it is today that American flight crews are undertaking aerial voyages of exploration, carrying the American flag over the seas and into the airports of the world, assuring for our Nation its place in the aerial commerce of the future. And, to our utter sadness, one of those crews has not returned.

And yet, they have not left us. Ed Musick's smile, his gentle personality, his marvelous skill in handling an airplane, will be with us always, encouraging us to complete the establishment of the Pacific air routes as he would have done it himself.

Let us, as friends, find comfort and courage in his memory.

Leslie, as Division Engineer, wrote a hand written letter to the parents of the young flight engineer, John Stickrod, who was lost with the Samoan Clipper. He sent this typewritten copy to his colleagues so they would know that he had expressed on behalf of Pan American its deep regret for the loss of their son.

PAA PAN AMERICAN AIRWAYS COMPANY

PERSONAL
for

COL. C. M. YOUNG
MR. C. T. RAMSEY
MR. P. MITCHELL
MR. ANDRE PRIESTER
MR. PHIL BERST

1-13-1938
Copies of letter (handwritten) sent by Mr. John C. Leslie to Mr. and Mrs. Stickrod (J.) at Los Angeles

"My dear Mr. and Mrs. Stickrod -

There is nothing I can say which will repair the loss we have all suffered in the death of your son. I am sure you know that we who were associated with him in his work extend to you our sincerest sympathy.

I think you will want to know how much of a place he had made for himself during his relatively short time with our Company. The position he held was one of real importance, which is in itself clear evidence of his proficiency. More than that, he was notable always for irreproachable conduct and enthusiastic loyalty to his organization.

Your loss, and ours, is a great one. I only hope that we may all find comfort in the fact that he died doing that which he most loved to do, and in a project of manifest importance to our Nation.

Sincerely,

John C. Leslie.

San Francisco
January 14, 1938"

PAN AMERICAN AIRWAYS SYSTEM—GENERAL OFFICES—135 E. 42ND STREET, NEW YORK CITY

Leslie reviewed the records of the maintenance of the plane and noted that the fuel dumping valve maintenance had not been signed off. He sent a strong message of disapproval to responsible parties at the Pacific bases. He was confident that this had not been the cause of the accident, but pointed out that maintenance instructions could be questioned, but never ignored.

> Upon investigating the maintenance records of NC-16734, we were much perturbed to find that the prescribed dump valve tests had not regularly been made. This test was called for both on the printed form used in Manila and on the mimeographed form used during the airplane's last service in Honolulu. The test had apparently not been made, or at any rate the item had not been signed off, for several months past. To the best of our recollection, there had never been any request to this office for permission to omit the item.
>
> As a matter of practical fact, we are thoroughly convinced that the failure to perform this item's work had no bearing whatsoever on the accident to the airplane. The omission of the item on the work order has not yet caused any embarrassment in the Bureau of Air Commerce investigation, although it has not yet terminated and we have no idea whether or not the question will ultimately be raised.
>
> The important point is that a maintenance procedure specifically requested by this office has not been carried out, that the failure to execute the item was not brought to the attention of this office, and that no request was made for an amendment or omission of the item. We have repeatedly stated that our orders are subject to question and discussion at all times, except in accute emergencies. In making that statement, however, we have remarked with equal vigor that our orders must either be carried out or questioned, but never simply ignored. The present incident illustrates in very painful fashion why our stated policy must be understood, remembered, and observed by all members of the Maintenance Department.

Condolences poured in from around the globe; this one from England was typical.

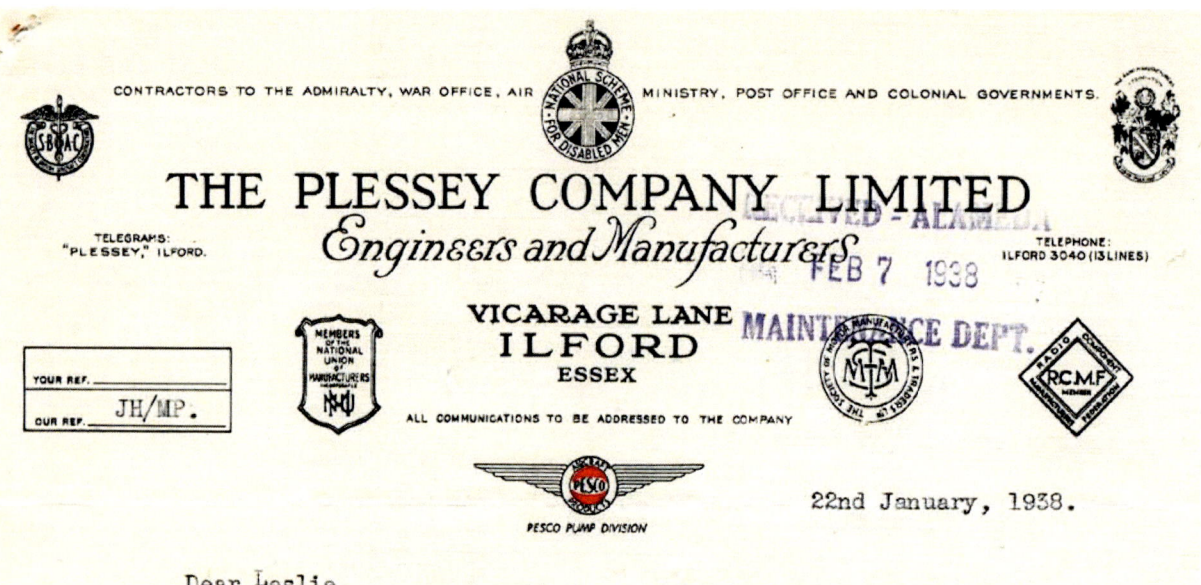

THE PLESSEY COMPANY LIMITED
Engineers and Manufacturers

VICARAGE LANE
ILFORD
ESSEX

OUR REF. JH/MP.

22nd January, 1938.

Dear Leslie,

Words fail me in this attempt to express my deep regrets over the recent misfortune on the Pacific Division. The news filtered through via the daily press and I just want to let you know that even though we are some 6,000 miles apart I was terribly distressed. I trust however, that we in this flying game can take the bitter with the sweet.

CHAPTER 5
"A MOST SHOCKING AND INCREDIBLE MYSTERY"

Six months after the loss of the *Samoan Clipper*, the *Hawaii Clipper* disappeared between Guam and Manila. Suddenly radio contact was lost and, in spite of an extensive search, not a trace of the plane, or its crew of nine and six passengers was ever found. Historians still wonder what happened.

New York World-Telegram — NEW YORK, FRIDAY, JULY 29, 1938.

PACIFIC CLIPPER MISSING WITH 15

The Evening Star — WASHINGTON, D. C., SATURDAY, JULY 30, 1938

OIL PATCH FOUND ON COURSE OF CLIPPER

THE SUN — BALTIMORE, SATURDAY, JULY 30, 1938

SHIP FAILS TO FIND CLIPPER

THE BALTIMORE NEWS-POST — SATURDAY, JULY 30, 1938

The Hawaii Clipper's pilot, Captain Leo Terletzky, was a Russian who came to the United States after being on the losing side of the Russian Revolution of 1917. He married Sarepta Bowman, a graduate of Smith College, who at the start of World War II joined the newly formed WAVES and became a Captain in the United States Navy. John and Jean Leslie were social friends of Leo and Serepta in Miami and San Francisco.

The two principal theories on the fate of plane and its crew were that it was hijacked by Japanese stowaways who wanted to capture the state-of-the-art flying boat to copy its marvelous Twin Wasp engines and all its other advanced equipment. The second theory is that the plane suffered a catastrophic structural failure in turbulent air.

Leslie's view at the time was that the cause of the disappearance was a "most incredible and shocking mystery" as evidenced by this letter to a Pan American colleague. He did not change his mind over the years.

> **PERSONAL**
>
> Mr. E. P. Critchley
> Pan American Airways, Inc.
> Miami, Florida
>
> Dear Ed:
>
> Thanks ever so much for your letter of August 2nd. The loss of the Hawaii Clipper remains a most incredible and shocking mystery. I enjoyed a somewhat personal friendship with Leo, as you know, which has intensified my distress and which, at the same time, led me to appreciate particularly the first paragraph of your letter.

This letter was written by Leslie August 9, 1938. Critchley's letter to Leslie was not found.

Leslie's papers contain a two-page memo to Col. Young, Pacific Division Manager, dated a month before the loss of the aircraft referring to reports that the Glenn L Martin Co. had written the Bureau of Air Commerce stating that the M-130 aircraft were "unairworthy" until all the sea wing (sponson) struts had been changed. The memo is technical in nature but Leslie felt emphatically that his professional reputation had been questioned and that the Martin company's actions and opinions were without merit. The discussion of the problem of the struts had been going on since the previous year and Leslie wanted to know what Martin was going to do about "reinforcement."

This memo concludes that the debate and the solution had nothing to do with the airworthiness of the aircraft, but rather the integrity of the sea wing that might fail on a hard water landing.

Leslie's files also contain a short, handwritten memo to Col. Young dated a few weeks after the loss of the clipper that states,

> *I have reason to believe that the representatives of the Martin Co. are exceedingly active at Buraircom (Bureau of Air Commerce) now in an effort to pin the loss of NC14 on faulty maintenance. I recommend and request that we take active measures to defend ourselves against this contemptible conduct.*

Pan Am historian, Jon Krupnick, reading these memos in recent years exclaimed, "Now I know why Pan American never did any more business with Martin."

The Bureau of Air Commerce launched an investigation of the loss of the Hawaii Clipper and concluded that the plane was airworthy and the crew physically and technically fit, and that the cause of the disappearance could not be ascertained.

Personal

June 30, 1938

Division Manager　　　　　　　　　　　　Division Engineer

Pacific　　　　　　　　　　　　　　　　　Pacific

Alameda　　　　　　　　　　　　　　　　 Alameda

Glenn L. Martin Company

      I understood from you on the telephone that the Glenn L. Martin Company had written a letter to the Bureau of Air Commerce stating that our Martin 130 airplanes were "unairworthy" until all of the struts had been changed to the new type material.

      If this statement is approximately correct, I cannot avoid the conclusion that my professional reputation has been placed very much in question and that I must take corresponding exception to any such statement from the Glenn L. Martin Company.

      In brief, there is no single shred of evidence to support any such statement. If there were any basis for the premise, it was certainly destroyed by the strut failure experienced on NC14 yesterday. We say this because the strut which failed yesterday was manufactured from the so-called new, improved material. Furthermore, the nature of the failure was nearly identical with that suffered by the same strut in the same location on the same airplane on September 22, 1937. This is illustrated in the attached photograph. Finally, Mr. Beecher quite independently gave us an analysis of the failure which was very similar to that found in our memorandum of October 20th to the Chief Engineer, a copy of which Mr. Beecher had never seen.

      In a memo of October 20, 1937 to the Chief Engineer we made the statement "..... one must conclude that the design of the unit did not provide enough strength for the particular combination of loads occurring at that moment".

      Our air-mail-gram of November 29, 1937 to the Chief Engineer read as follows:

      "We remain totally unconvinced that our two seawing jury strut failures were due to a failure of the strut material occasioned by faulty manufacturing processes and consequent built-in stresses. On the contrary, and until satisfactory evidence is offered otherwise, we will continue to believe that those two failures were due to an accidental loading beyond the capacity of the strut to absorb it.

      "In view of this, we remain very uneasy about the present design and we continue more than anxious to know what the Glenn L. Martin Company proposes to do about a re-inforcement. We have of course discussed this in previous memoranda and anxiously await your decision."

- 2 -

In our memo of December 21, 1937 to the Chief Engineer we brought out the following points:

1. The Martin seawing stress analysis used an assumed load equal to the displacement of the seawing multiplied by a load factor of four, distributed over the bottom in an arbitrary fashion, not substantiated by further calculations or references.

2. A letter of May 7, 1936 from the Glenn L. Martin Company to the Chief Engineer included the phrases "Furthermore, we had had no experience with the type of loads occurring on seawings" and "Based on this and other similar difficulties we now would not use the same type of connection".

3. Our memorandum included the phrase "We believe that the forward seawing supporting structure is insufficiently strong to withstand reasonably severe operating conditions, simply because the original assumption in the stress analysis is not correct".

It disturbs me greatly to think that both the Company's reputation and my own are being jeopardized by a statement which finds so little support in the actual facts of the case. I should be most grateful for anything which you could do to remedy the situation.

John C. Leslie
Division Engineer

MEMORANDUM Personal

TO Div. Mgr.
FROM Div. Engineer
DATE Aug. 16, 1938
SUBJECT Glenn L. Martin Co.

I have reason to believe that the representatives of the Martin Co. are exceedingly active at Buaircom now, in an effort to pin the loss of NC14 on faulty maintenance.

I recommend and request that we take active measures to defend ourselves against this contemptible conduct.

Thanks!

John C. Leslie

PML NOTE 3/25/2011 BUREAU AIR COMM. REQUEST "AIRWORTHY" DATE? 17 AUG 38 INQUIRY STARTED

Years later, people were still debating, speculating and even inventing "true stories," on what happened.

In 1980, Pan Am VP James Arey contacted Leslie and other veterans to gather their recollections. Pan Am wanted to refute assertions about the disappearance in a book entitled *The China Clipper* by Ronald Jackson, subtitled *The True Story of the Pan American Flying Boats....* The book was at times sloppily written and highly speculative. Pan Am thought the "true story" of the disappearance of the Hawaii Clipper was completely unsubstantiated.

> In a 1980 letter James Arey wrote concerning certain airplane wreckage found at Truk.

```
As to looking into the wreckage at Truk, a panel
of Pan Am pilots, flight engineers, aeronautical
engineers, mechanics and myself have thoroughly examined
the photos and related material submitted by Mr. Gervais,
and found that the aircraft in question was definitely
NOT a Martin 130 flying boat.
```

> Also in 1980, Leslie wrote to VP Arey.

Juan Trippe was always convinced that the airplane was hi-jacked by the Japanese for the sake of the technology aboard in the engine. He used to cite the fact that Admiral Towers in his post-war investigations in Japan claimed to have found some magnetos on Japanese engines with the same serial numbers as were on the Hawaii Clipper. Whenever I taxed Mr. Trippe with the fact that there was no written record of this whatsoever, that I could find, he simply evaded the subject, insisting that it was so. I was an intimate friend of Admiral Towers when he was with Pan Am after the War and lunched with him on frequent occasions, reminiscing about World War II. He never mentioned any such affair at all to me.

> Leslie goes on in the same letter.   (Author's note: the word Leslie dictated was almost certainly "cumulonimbus" not "CumuLimbus")

As I remember the last weather report from the airplane, it was flying in a solid overcast at some 7,000 feet (memory (?). No distress message of any kind was ever received. It was characteristic of weather in that area to show heavy solid overcast with very large thunder clouds penetrating through the overcast. My own theory, for want of a better one, is that they flew under the overcast into heavy vertical turbulence of a CumuLimbus and either lost control or suffered a structural failure due to heavy acceleration, perhaps more likely the latter. Personally, with absolutely no negative engineering evidence, I have always wondered whether one of the one of the wires on the wire-braced tail might have parted company. An extensive search was conducted by sea, mostly through the U.S. Navy, and oil slicks were investigated but never any that matched fluids on board the Hawaii Clipper.

Veteran Pan American flying boat Captain Robert Ford had this to say about flying the M-130 in turbulent weather with its single tail, which may bolster Leslie's speculation about horizontal and vertical stabilizers guyed by eight wires possibly failing. In any event, if Captain Terletsky did hit unexpected, severe turbulence, he might have had the same trouble controlling the aircraft that Captain Ford described in an interview on film made in about 2000 by Doug Miller of Pelican Films.

I was flying out of Honolulu on a Martin M-130 with a load of dependents and children of the military. And I climbed up to the old Hilo intersection, and leveled off, and we were in the soup, and it was cold. It was sleeting and snowing, and zero visibility, and . . It got rough, plenty rough. And with that single tail, instead of the three tails that the B-314's have, just that single tail, it was like a hot knife cutting butter.

So, it was a rough ride. Eighteen hours later we ended up back at Honolulu where we started. The vomit was running in the aisle! Boy, it was a mess, oh! It was a mess. But I never did like that M-130 on instruments in rough air with that single rudder, no.

Captain Ford was particularly famous for having been en route to New Zealand piloting a Boeing B-314 when the Japanese bombed Pearl Harbor. He continued around the world to the west, crossing the Australian continent, the Indian Ocean, Arabia, Africa and the Atlantic Ocean to Brazil before turning north for a surprise arrival at New York City. The account of this voyage is one of the most gripping, imaginative and courageous exploits in Pan American history, and there are plenty to choose from!

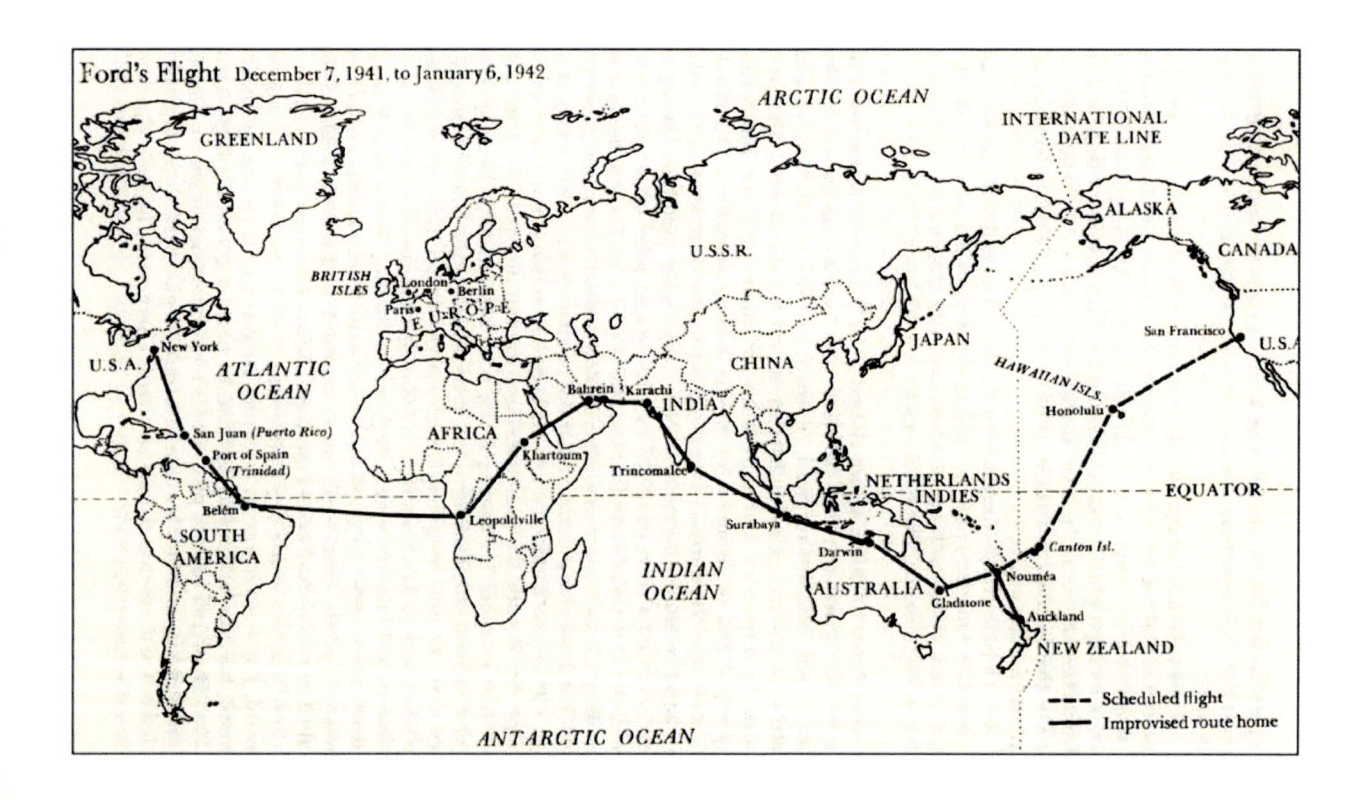

Ford's Flight December 7, 1941, to January 6, 1942

THE MIGHTY, MARVELOUS BOEING 314

by John McCoy, 1962

Leslie and his colleagues waited impatiently to get more and newer planes to supplement the small fleet of three Martin M-130s and a few S42s in the Pacific. Neither Martin nor Sikorsky were interested, but Boeing had a XB-15 bomber that was not going into production and they could use its newly designed wing and powerful engines. They would have to design a seaplane fuselage. An order was placed in the spring of 1936, promised for 1937, but were only delivered in 1938. The first on-the-water test on Puget Sound on a very windy day was nearly a disaster as the plane almost capsized. The sea wings had to be adjusted, among other things. The first test flight was also scary as the plane would only fly in a straight line. The pilot had to increase and decrease engine speed on one side to control the direction. Boeing added two vertical stabilizers, shown on their next year's holiday card. There was a certain amount of trial and error in manufacturing these early aircraft. For the B-314 there was more to come.

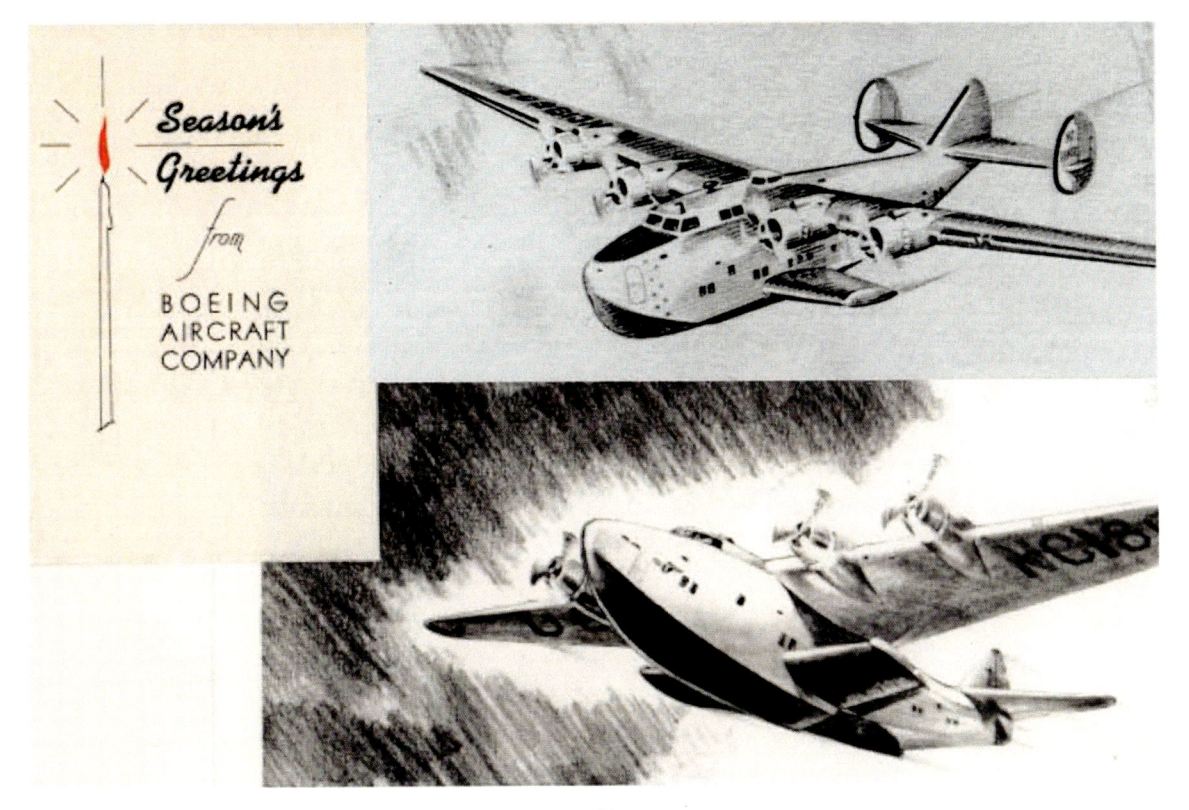

Problems to solve were myriad, but Leslie and his colleagues worked closely with Boeing to make the B-314 the most advanced and comfortable long range aircraft in the world. This process is best summed up in a letter to him from Boeing engineer Wellwood Beall written in 1974.

> You will also recall during the Boeing tests that the aircraft had very large dutch roll tendencies and it was for this reason that we added fins and rudders on the ends of the stabilizers and took the rudder off the middle. This was because we had left too much dihedral in the wings with the center of gravity so low. This change caused structural difficulties in the horizontal stabilizer. We sent George Martin who was head of our Structural Department to Treasure Island and he installed strain gauges. These recorded 24 gs on landing and so we had to reinforce the bending strength of the horizontal stabilizer.

Then there was the issue of porpoising — bouncing back into the air after touch down.

> I remember in the very early days after our first delivery and our proving trip to the Orient, André Priester asked me to go to San Francisco and bring Earl Ferguson, a Boeing pilot with me, for the purposes of demonstrating the taking off and landing the flying boat without porpoising. Earl as pilot and I as copilot had no trouble. However, the boat flown by the Pan Am pilots always skipped on landing. Earl and I overcame this problem by chopping the throttles just a second before we touched the water. Neither you nor André were satisfied with this technique and Priester insisted I stay for another day. This was the day that the Stratoliner crashed on a KLM demonstration flight. Thus, André saved my life as all on board were killed.

Robert Daley wrote in AMERICAN SAGA about the porpoising:

> **After all this, a year late in delivery, the first Boeing was flown to San Francisco, where it was taken out for test flights over San Francisco Bay. William Cluthe, an experienced Pan Am flying-boat captain, was at the controls. Cluthe kept bouncing the flying boat off the water. He was embarrassed because he thought it was his fault. But no matter how he tried he couldn't make the hull stick without bouncing. Aboard were Leslie, now Pacific operations manager, and Wellwood Beall, the Boeing project engineer. Leslie took Beall back into the stern of the aircraft to tell him in a quiet voice that this "porpoising" simply wouldn't do. The airplane was unacceptable.**

Beall goes on to say:

> I remember the porpoising and the skipping were finally and easily solved by extending the step on the boat twenty inches. You will recall during the Boeing test flight, we had put three degrees dihedral in the sponsons.

Beall sums up, the end result:

> What we should really do is tell about the good things as well, such as the dining salon, the spiral stairway, the cruise quarters, the honeymoon suite, the flushing toilet, the largest commercial aircraft in the world at that time, etc.

Indeed, they had accomplished their goal and Boeing produced 12 of these mighty aircraft. Pan American continued to improve its Pacific service, fly across the Atlantic and play an important part in World War II with nine of these planes as the backbone of its fleet. The British, already at war, had a dire need for the range and cargo capacity of these flying boats. President Roosevelt directed that three be sold to them for their war effort.

Leslie kept in his papers a humorous example of the intensity of the effort to perfect the Boeing B-314. As engineers of the two companies labored in Seattle and San Francisco several inter-company romances developed, which led Boeing to protest, tongue in cheek.

> The Boeing Company is very much perturbed at Pan American Personnel taking possession of their Company property without necessary authority.
>
> Understand Junior Engineer Taylor has arranged to take with him, on or about May 15, Miss Pat Reisel who is an outstanding asset in the Accounting Department.
>
> Also, we have learned indirectly that Junior Engineer Borger is planning to appropiate, sometime in the near future, Miss Muriel Hannah, also a priceless asset in the Engineering Department.
>
> Things of this nature cannot be tolerated without proper release by all parties concerned. To prevent future embarrassment it will be greatly appreciated if you will keep away from this assignment all eligible PAA bachelors.

Leslie and unidentified flight crew member confer aboard a Boeing B-314.

Leslie's lapel pin for ten years of service.

"THERE'S YOUR LAND, BOYS"

In the absence of permission from Australia fly to that larger market, Trippe decided to force the issue by flying to New Zealand, whose government was willing to give permission even though they had no aircraft able to fly a reciprocal route to the United States. In August of 1939, as Europe teetered on the edge of World War II, Leslie, Operations Manager of the Pacific Division, planned and flew the new route. This time the dangerous harbor of Pago Pago, Samoa, was bypassed as was the awkward base at Kingman Reef, which had only of few hundred square yards of dry land that required a supply vessel anchored in the lagoon. Instead, a new seaplane base at Canton Island had been built and the second refueling stop was in Noumea, New Caledonia, a French colony.

THE NEW ZEALAND HERALD, THURSDAY, AUGUST 31, 1939

ARRIVAL OF CLIPPER

FLIGHT FROM NOUMEA

LANDING AT AUCKLAND

GREETED BY GREAT CROWDS

DEPARTURE NEXT SATURDAY

OVER THE CITY

FIRST VIEW OF CRAFT

SWIFT DESCENT MADE

ONE HARBOUR CIRCUIT

IMPRESSIVE PICTURE

Even to those who had watched the arrival of big flying-boats at Auckland on earlier occasions, the advent of the huge California Clipper yesterday afternoon was something likely to remain long in memory. The thousands who gathered on the eastern waterfront had expected to see a gigantic aircraft, but the reality exceeded their hopes. She seemed hardly to belong to the present, but rather to the domain of things to come, so often depicted by imaginative artists in the pages of magazines.

Hardly less wonderful than the craft herself was the skill and sureness with which she was flown around the harbour and finally was brought down to rest on its waters, almost as easily as a small seaplane.

The people of Auckland, New Zealand, remembering fondly the first Pan American survey flight in 1937 and famous Captain Ed Musick, turned out in force to welcome the flight and to see the world's mightiest airplane.

Accentuating the importance of the Pacific routes and long-range, over-ocean aircraft, on board were representatives of the US government as well as officers from the Army Air Corps, Navy, and Coast Guard,. These new Boeing B-314s were soon to be hugely important in the coming war with Japan and Germany.

Leslie liked to tell the story of the arrival at New Zealand. He described himself as "kibitzing" on the spacious flight deck as they approached in challenging weather conditions.

P.A.A. (B314) Flight Deck Showing Crew — La Guardia Field

We were approaching the north cape of New Zealand, which is a strip of rather high hills, maybe 200 feet high, which form a barricade for a width of some 50 miles. Off to starboard were some rather high mountain islands called the Three Kings. The weather was extremely gray and murky with rain, and we were consequently flying over the ocean at about 800 to 1000 feet. Knowing these obstacles were somewhere ahead, but in the absence of radio navigation at that time, not being to sure of where they were, we were all in the cockpit peering forward through the windshield.

We were not in a dangerous condition, but were hoping to make our landfall with a reasonable margin, All of a sudden I noticed through the windshield a long white cloud standing out against the gray murky background and, as anyone would who knows about weather and terrain, I said, 'There's your land, boys!' and we made the cape pretty soon after that.

I was telling that story to the Mayor of Auckland, New Zealand at a reception a couple of nights later and he stopped me in the middle and said, 'Did you say long white cloud*,' Mr. Leslie?' and I said, 'Yes, Sir, why?' He said, 'That is the literal translation of the Maori name for New Zealand: Aotearoa.'*

In other words, the Maoris paddling canoes down from the North from whence they emigrated undoubtedly saw the same weather that we saw coming in in our flying machine.

California Clipper and a British Short flying boat in Auckland Harbor, New Zealand

67

Leslie rubs noses with a Maori Princess welcoming him to Aotearoa.

Four U. S. aviation officials are trying to explain to their wives these days that many strange customs exist in some parts of the world and that the old adage, "When in Rome do as the Romans do" held good in the interior of New Zealand recently. It seems that the Americans on board the PAA California Clipper on its maiden flight to Auckland were taken 175 miles into the heart of New Zealand to visit the Maoris, a group of people who settled there about 600 years ago and who originally came from Hawaii. Prior to being escorted through the tribal lands the Americans were met by a Maori princess and according to the custom of the Maori, the princess greets visitors by rubbing noses.

NEW SERVICE

PASSENGER TRIPS

EARLY START EXPECTED

FORTNIGHTLY SCHEDULE

ROOM FOR 36 PEOPLE

While the inauguration of the air passenger service from San Francisco to Auckland is subject to the approval of the United States Civil Aeronautics Authority, Pan American Airways hope to be able to commence this within a matter of weeks, according to Mr. J. C. Leslie, operations manager for the Pacific division of the company's services. The company was virtually ready to begin ordinary passenger flights on the route, he added.

MR. J. C. LESLIE

ROUTINE FLYING

UNEVENTFUL JOURNEY

ACCURATE NAVIGATION

NORFOLK ISLAND VIEWED

Characterised by routine efficiency, the survey flight of the Boeing Clipper over the new ocean route of nearly 8000 miles was completed "without a bump." The only adverse weather was experienced off the New Zealand coast yesterday, when driving rain squalls and a strong north-westerly wind were encountered.

CHAPTER 6
"IT ALL SEEMS UTTERLY INSANE"

Leslie wrote in his memoirs about the overnight stop for refueling on the Canton Island base and hearing of the start of World War II:

Coming north from New Zealand we were on Canton Island the night when war broke out in Europe ... 'The Guns of August.' I remember so vividly listening to some of the high frequency radio broadcasts coming through the tropical static so we had at least a faint grasp of what was going on. I was old enough to have a distinct recollection of World War I, with three older brothers in the Armed Forces, so I could think of all that while facing the prospect of World War II, which we all knew it would be. I remember lying in my bunk and thinking of my wife and three young children, wondering when America would be drawn in and when I would be called to active duty as a long-time officer in Naval Reserves. I tried to visualize what it would mean for Pan American World Airways in the way of wartime duties. It never occurred to me that I would be in New York as Manager of the Atlantic Division by the time of Pearl Harbor, 7 December 1941.

Leslie kept in his papers a sole newspaper clipping from late 1935 about German persecutions of Jews and Catholics. In 1938, the year of both Kristallnacht and the disastrous Munich Conference, he received a letter on the next page from Otto Julius Merkel, one of the founders of Lufthansa.

SECRET POLICE SEIZE "JEWISH NAZI" HEAD

Union Ordered Disbanded—Catholic Bishop Fined $40,240 or Three Months in Jail.

By Jewish Telegraphic Agency.

BERLIN, Nov. 23.—Dr. Max Naumann, president of the Union of Nationalist Jewish Germans, today was arrested by the Gestapo Nazi secret police. The union comprising the so-called "Jewish Nazis" was officially ordered disbanded yesterday.

A blacklist of Jewish composers and musicians dating back to 1780 was issued today.

By the United Press.

BERLIN, Nov. 23.—Dr. Peter Legge, Catholic Bishop of Meissen, was sentenced today to pay a fine of $40,240 or to serve three months in jail on conviction of violating German laws restricting transactions in foreign exchange.

Bishop Legge is the first clergyman of his rank to face a German court in sixty years. He also is the highest ranking Catholic among the dozens of his faith who recently have been prosecuted on similar charges.

By the Associated Press.

MUNICH, Germany, Nov. 23.—Police closed Catholic libraries here today "to examine their contents for forbidden books."

OTTO JULIUS MERKEL BERLIN W9 30/9/1938
Columbus Haus · Potsdamer Platz 1
Telefon: 21 31 06
Kabel-Anschrift: Hansamer Berlin

Dear Mr. Leslie,

Everybody's heart is filled with gratitude about the good sense that has prevailed in Munich, expressing the feeling of all the people of England, France, Germany, Italy and the United States and in Fract of the entire world. The four statesmen have truly interpreted our innermost wishes.

We in Germany have been particularly struck with the character shown by Neville Chamberlain. He justly quoted, on leaving Heston for Munich, Hotspur's words in Henry IV:

"I tell you, my Lord Fool:
Out of this nettle, danger,
We pluck this flower, safety."

Sincerely yours,

John C. Leslie, Esq.
San Francisco, Cal.

Merkel and Leslie may have met in South America as German airlines were crossing the South Atlantic during the early 1930's.

Merkel must have written another letter to Leslie in mid-1939, but it was not found. Here are the principal paragraphs of Leslie's replies of January and December, 1939.

One sees that Leslie was already pessimistic about the coming-to-power of the NAZI government, its implication for world peace and for "tolerance and reason."

To John Leslie, whose family had benefited from America's religious freedom and individual opportunity, events in Europe were "utterly insane."

I wish that I could, in all honesty, share your gratification concerning the results of the Munich Conference. I am afraid, however, that many of us in this Country are deeply concerned over some of the tendencies which we see in the world today. In our Country, as well as in others, we seem to see a growing tendency toward "absolutism", wherein the common people are either influenced or constrained to act emotionally, guided neither by good logic nor by the principles of human kindliness and cooperation. I only hope that in the New Year we may all have new opportunity to realise the virtues of tolerance and reason.

Many of us in America feel that our unhappiness over events in Europe is rivaled only by our confusion as to the methods and conflicts of the various nations. To many of us it all seems utterly insane. Perhaps that is because we have spent too many generations magnifying the importance of the individual and diminishing the importance of the state. I think I know the people of my country well enough to say that they will not soon learn to depreciate the rights of the individual, and they will not soon be in a mental attitude favorable to the acquisition of new territory on this continent. I am puzzled by your failure to mention Japan as a factor of much interest to the world today.

"1935-1941 WERE GOLDEN"

Leslie wrote in his memoirs about his work and his family's love of San Francisco:

The six pre-war years we spent in the Pacific Division, 1935-1941, were 'Golden.' My work was fascinating beyond measure, and San Francisco was the most glorious city in the world in which to live. We made many good friends there and felt as though we could spend the rest of our lives right there. But then came the customary event in big corporations. We had (foolishly, I suppose) built a new house out toward Walnut Creek, at Lafayette, California. They were just putting the wallpaper on the house when I was summoned to New York and invited to become Manager of Pan Am's Atlantic Division. This was in the fall of 1940.

I remember sitting at Juan Trippe's desk in the Chrysler Building one evening about 6 o'clock discussing the move and asking, 'Mr. Trippe, can anybody really live like a human being in the New York area?' He gravely assured me that they could (he having lived in New York all his life). It was not that we were so ignorant of New York. We had been married at the Princeton University Chapel and had started our married life in Rye, New York, but after San Francisco we questioned whether anybody could live decently anywhere else. After spending an hour in her new kitchen, never used, weeping silently, my gallant wife accepted the challenge with me and East we came.

Leslie's colleagues gave him a cherished memento, an original blade of the China Clipper, engraved with his dates of service and jobs held in the Pacific Division. Black and white positive photos of the Sikorsky S-42, the China Clipper and the Boeing B-314 glowed warmly in the shade and attracted attention on Leslie's desk for the next forty years.

Colonel Young, on the right, wrote a glowing letter of thanks for Leslie's contribution to the success of Pan American in the pioneering of the Pacific routes.

Mr. Leslie's record with the Pacific Division is one of outstanding industry and accomplishment. He has b en an important guiding force in the development of the trans-Pacific route, both to the Orient and Australasia, in building up the Division organization, and in evolving the fundamental policies, practices, and technique of long-range operation, without which scheduled transocean services could not be successfully conducted.

"MY NEW DIVISION WAS AT WAR"

Leslie wrote in his memoirs:

I have been trying to remember when it first struck me that we in Pan American were effectively part of World War II. From the time of our arrival in the Pacific Division early in 1935, my wife and I became more and more sensitized to the war clouds looming over the Pacific. It was apparent to many people on the West Coast, interested in foreign affairs, that Japan was becoming a threat—a fact of which we never could convince our friends on the East Coast, until Pearl Harbor. Actually, as we were pushing the Pan American route across the Pacific to Manila and Hong Kong, the Japanese government was voicing official objections, claiming that this was a warlike move on the part of the United States.

President Juan Trippe welcomes new Atlantic Division Manager Leslie to the Marine Air Terminal at North Beach, LaGuardia Field.

Admiral Leahy, United States Chief of Naval Operations and later five star Fleet Admiral testified about Pan American's importance to the national interest

"In the first place, Pan American Airways' activities from the beginning have been of great value to the Navy. Its pioneering work in equipment, methods, development of routes, establishment of aids to seaplane operations, and opening up of foreign territory to air activity, has done far more than can be measured in concrete terms to assist naval aviation in its own development and progress. For this reason and because of Pan American's continuing close cooperation with the Navy, and its eagerness always to make available to the Navy its facilities, information and assistance, its problems merit all practicable support from the Navy Department in all interests of national defense."

Leslie continues:

By the time I was transferred to the Atlantic Division as Division Manager in January 1941, I was personally convinced that my new Division was at war and that my assignment would have little to do with tourism, commercial marketing, or any of the peacetime challenges.

For over a year the beleaguered Pan Am representatives in Lisbon, Portugal, had been fending off the indescribable pressure of refugees seeking to flee from Europe to find haven anywhere in the Western Hemisphere. President Roosevelt's Neutrality Proclamation had driven Pan American out of the United Kingdom, and temporarily out of Ireland as well. This left for the time being only the Pan Am service to Portugal.

The bizarre feature of Lisbon was the presence of the Germans and the Japanese. To find oneself crowded into a tiny jewelry store during the war, back to back with Japanese and Germans, was peculiar to say the least. Also, to go out to the Lisbon airport and see a Lufthansa aircraft arrive, followed closely by a British Overseas Airlines (BOAC) DC-3 gave one an almost unreal feeling.

Yankee Clipper arrives in Lisbon, 1939

Leslie goes on:

Meanwhile, two other Divisions of the company, Pan American Air Ferries and the Airport Development Program were involved in wartime activities, also long before Pearl Harbor. I recall the contract was being negotiated in Washington—a very secret one—whereby Pan American would build a chain of airports in the Caribbean, Central America, and South America. Likewise, Pan American Air Ferries was transporting combat aircraft across the South Atlantic, Africa and beyond in support of the British forces.

neral Delos C. Emmons, Commanding General, General Headquarters, US Army Air said this about Pan American's vital role:

The economic and military value of the Pan American Airways System to the United States and its broad concept of military defense cannot be overestimated. . . . The concentration of Air Force units from North America into South America will depend solely in the existing circumstances, on the full utilization of Pan American.

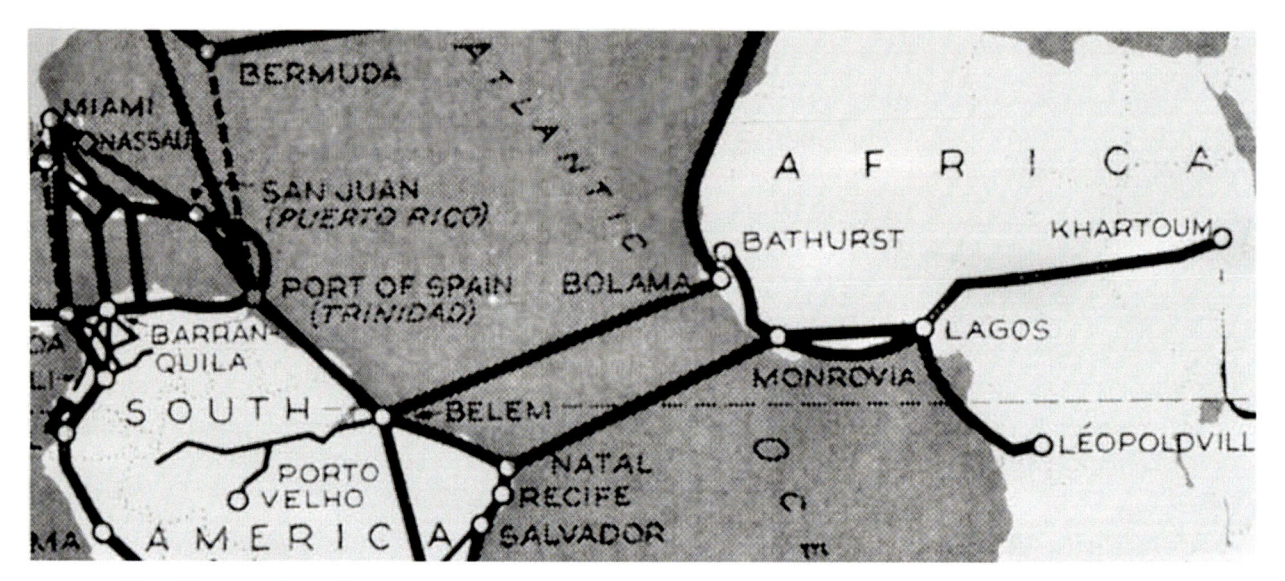

Leslie continued:

The Atlantic Division was also preparing in the summer of 1941 to mount an ostensibly commercial scheduled air service with Boeing flying boats from New York via Brazil and West Africa to Leopoldville, in what was then called the Belgian Congo. The most immediate task was to build a base at Fisherman's Lake, Liberia, without which it would have been very difficult to assure a safe landfall on the West African coast, an adequate fueling and maintenance facility, and a distribution point for cargo and personnel. The Atlantic Division managed the building of the seaplane base at Fisherman's Lake, Liberia.

In the later case of the new land airport at Santa Maria in the Azores, the Atlantic Division was the front for what was really an Army Engineers Corps operation. I well remember having some of my active-duty friends come to my office at LaGuardia to arrange this project and my signing them both on to the Pan Am payroll at $1 per year. We bought several hundred pairs of khaki coveralls with PAA stenciled on the back, which in fact were to garb U.S. Government personnel (soldiers, I believe.)

In July 1941, Karl Lueder, Assistant Operations Manager of Pan-Africa, and an old Pacific Division hand, went by boat from Monrovia to Fisherman's Lake (variously known as Cape Mount or Robertsport). Lueder surveyed Fisherman's Lake to determine its suitability for flying boat operations. He found it excellent and planning for the Congo service went ahead

Fisherman's Lake

with Fisherman's Lake as its anchor on the west Coast of Africa. A Clipper went into Fisherman's Lake to pick up Lueder. A survey flight was planned to Leopoldville. I decided that both I and my colleague and friend, Ed McVitty, the Assistant Division Manager, should accompany this trip. I recall McVitty and me being carried ashore on Liberian shoulders into high grass, where the poisonous green Mamba snake was not unknown. Grass was all there was.

We decided that this was an excellent location for the seaplane docking facility and consequently for the adjoining camp. None of this would have

Clearing the landplane runway at Fisherman's Lake

been possible, at least not so rapidly and efficiently, had it not been for a remarkable Episcopal missionary and his wife stationed at Cape Mount. Father Harvey Simmons was not only a fine man but also an excellent mechanic and boatman. He had a small motor launch which he allowed us to use for surveying the lake and for going ashore at the remote jungle point that we had selected for the cantonment. As soon as we could get back to Father Simmons's house, I originated a radio message to headquarters in New York asking 'full speed ahead' on construction of the Fisherman's Lake facility.

All of this preceded the negotiation of the contract establishing PAA Africa on 12 August 1941. That was a busy month! Four days later, the North Atlantic meeting took place between Churchill and Roosevelt. Six days later Roosevelt announced that PAA had agreed to undertake a project for the Government: (1) to establish a strategic air transport route between the United States and Africa. (2) to establish and maintain across Africa a second transport route linking those ports with key terminals in the Egyptian Sudan, and (3) to operate over this aerial highway a ferry service for combat aircraft.

Father Harvey Simmons

Two ships were en route to Bathurst (now Banjul, Gambia) at that time, one with some 30 construction men and the other with the prefabricated buildings and machinery necessary to build a camp. New York diverted both vessels to Fisherman's Lake through what, by that time, were seas dangerously infested by German submarines. Some 30 men landed on the beach at Fisherman's Lake (Cape Mount) on Christmas Eve 1941, with no one but the remarkable Father and Mrs. Simmons to feed and house them. McVitty and I had returned to New York to meet the next post-Pearl Harbor requirement.

It turned out that the principal function of this South American/African operation with the big flying boats of the Atlantic Division was to carry cargo from Natal to Fisherman's Lake and sometimes beyond to Lagos, and to transport ferry pilots back to the States for another flight of aircraft. However, there may have been a more immediate task, which was under the blanket of rigid wartime secrecy. I only know that when I flew back from Leopoldville (now Kinshasa) to America on the first flight, the main cabin floor was covered with small, heavy sacks of something labeled "beryllium". Knowing since then that the uranium for the American atomic experiment came from the Belgian Congo to Chicago's Argonne Laboratories, I have always supposed that we really brought back some of the first uranium.

Boeing B-314 at Fisherman's Lake, April, 1942

Leslie was invited by the Lieutenant Governor of the Belgian Congo to dinner the same day his Clipper arrived there, November 17, 1941.

Le Vice-Gouverneur Général
et Madame Paul Ermens
prient monsieur John C. Leslie

de leur faire l'honneur de dîner

chez eux le lundi 17 novembre 1941
à 19 heures 30.

R.S.V.P. Léopoldville, le 17 novembre 1941.

Atlantic Division Manager Leslie, wearing a white suit and a white pith helmet, confers with Belgian military and government officials in Leopoldville.

America's new lifeline to Africa

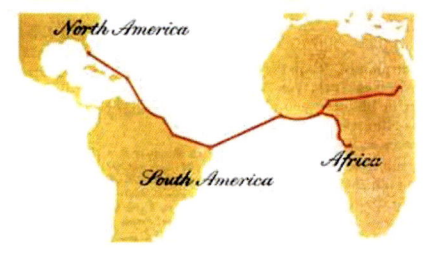

Leslie described in in his memoirs a crucial contribution made by Pan American personnel at a perilous time in World War II.

Pan American Airways-Africa, Limited, was being organized to build up the airway from West Africa to the Nile at Khartoum and down to Cairo, where the British forces were preparing in July 1942, to repel a major advance by Rommel's Afrika Korps. The British Eighth Army commanded by Montgomery found itself almost completely out of tank shell fuses. Seven planeloads with 15 tons of tank shell fuses were rushed to the front by PAA-Africa pilots to bring the desperate British artillery back into the game. The British victory in the Battle of El Alamein was a major turning point in the war. Thus the airfields we built and our pilots played their part in this turning of 'the hinge of fate,' — as it was later described by Winston Churchill.

Both images on this page are from a Pan American poster illustrating the contribution to the war effort.

A Boeing B-314 flying boat is overhead while Pan American Airways-Africa and British Royal Air Force landplanes await its precious cargo.

The Atlantic Division did what most of America did during the war - hire women to do what had been "a man's work." The results were excellent, to the surprise of many.

WAACS & WAVES

Atlantic Division Manager John C. Leslie has come forth with a declaration that apparently is the answer to the trials, the difficulties and, more important, the future of the WAVEs and WAACs -- the nation's unarmed forces in skirts. Manager Leslie recently returned from an inspection of Atlantic Division facilities in the British Isles.

"An American general at an airport near London complimented 125 WAAFs who are quartered at the base. 'These are the best soldiers I have ever had in my command,' the general remarked to me. And he enumerated the duties of the women who lead a rookie's life in airport barracks.

"In one English city I saw a WAAF, chauffeur to a civilian defense official, who had received her preliminary training as driver of a truck hauling unexploded bombs from wrecked streets," he stated.

Girls Take A Whirl As Mechanics, Tune Up And Shine Up Clippers

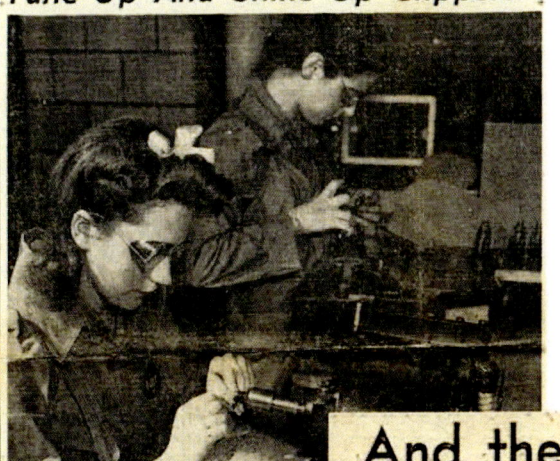

Pan American Airways Puts Girls in Men's Jobs

40 Are Assigned to Equipment Shops at LaGuardia Field

Pan American Airways has employed forty young women in its maintenance department at La-Guardia Field to perform tasks previously allotted to men, it was announced yesterday by the company's Atlantic division. Assignment of the new employees to the fabric and equipment shops has released an equal number of men for other duties.

The extraordinary growth of the Pan American system, which operates passenger, mail and express services by clipper to Europe, South America and Africa, and also performs pioneering surveys and ferry tasks for the government, has brought an increase in personnel in the Atlantic division from fifty-six in 1937 to 1,432 in 1942, of which 1,186 are based a LaGuardia Field. Indications are that as the service and maintenance forces of the company continue to grow, women will play an even larger role in the line's activities.

Plans are now being made to employ young women in the reservations-control department at La-Guardia Field, replacing men, and one young woman, Miss Vera M. D. Covell, has for several weeks been assigned to the flight-operations office, known as "flight watch," which relays clearance and landing instructions, weather and wind information to pilots approaching the field. Miss Covell, formerly a stenographer, holds a pilot's license, has completed a ground-instruction course and recently became a licensed operator of the radio telephone.

And the Male Workers' Morale Soars to a New High

CHAPTER 7
"NO BUZZ-BOMB FOUND ME THAT NIGHT"

LIFE Magazine, October 20, 1941, put this photograph of the Boeing B-314 on its large cover (10.5x14"). These airplanes, of which there were only a dozen, three of which were operated by the British, were already "an important item in U.S. defense plans.""

Leslie says in his memoirs:

Immediately at the time of Pearl Harbor, the Pan American flying boats were transferred to the ownership of the Navy, or the Army in one case. Contracts were entered into for the operation by Pan Am of these aircraft, both on the Atlantic and the Pacific, under the cognizance of the Naval Air Transport Service.

For all practical purposes, the Atlantic Division became a large squadron in the Atlantic Wing of NATS, whose headquarters were at Patuxent, MD. I had been a Naval Reserve officer since September, 1933, but the Navy chose to leave me at what I was doing, namely endeavoring to operate the Atlantic Division of Pan Am.

Although I went to Patuxent for staff meetings in civilian clothes, I was made to feel that I was just another Naval officer reporting operationally to the commander of the Atlantic Wing, Captain Syd Wildman, but still responsible to Pan Am headquarters for operation according to the contract and with due regard for Pan Am's property and financial interests.

I used three costumes during the War, sometimes on a single trip: civilian clothes for commercial duty, Naval Air Transport Service (NATS) for contract flights and naval uniform when proceeding according to Navy orders, which happened only once — taking the President to the Casablanca Conference.

LIFE'S COVER

Photographed a few minutes after its arrival at LaGuardia Field, with a swarm of Pan American mechanics preparing it for its next take-off, the four-motored Clipper on the cover is one of three which, since 1939, have made regular flights to Lisbon and back. Pan American is this week installing a new service to Africa which will be an important item in U. S. defense plans. For more news about this extraordinary airline, see a close-up of its founder and president, Juan Trippe, on page 110.

Leslie's travel records show several trips to Ireland and the United Kingdom and on one such trip he visited the newspaper where his father had been an apprentice.

THE TYRONE CONSTITUTION, FRIDAY, OCTOBER 9, 1942.

Atlantic Clipper at Foynes, 1944

Leslie wrote in his memoirs:

When I first visited London, it was via the Clipper to Foynes, thence by BOAC land aircraft, windows blacked out, to Bristol, and from there by train to London. I always stayed at the Ritz Hotel and soon learned my way in the blackout at night from Grosvenor Square, past the Ritz, and down Piccadilly and the Strand as far as the Savoy. It is so hard to convey the feeling of those blacked-out nights in London.

My principal emotion was profound admiration for the courage, morale, and self-discipline of the British people. The city had been badly hurt during the Blitz and firebombing. Food was scarce. Transportation was difficult. Yet work and war went forward with courage and good humor.

On a later trip over I rode on one of the Consolidated Coronados which had been given to us by the Navy to operate for their account. This flight was across the North

MANAGER OF CLIPPER SERVICE VISITS CONSTITUTION OFFICE.

Father Once Worked in "Con."

ON Wednesday, an interesting visitor to Ulster paid a visit to "The Tyrone Constitution" office. He was Mr. John C. Leslie, manager of the Atlantic Division Pan American Airways System, of New York, Baltimore (better known as the Clipper Service), which has done so much to develop air travel between Ireland and America.

Mr. Leslie was keenly interested in everything he saw in the office, as his father, who died in 1939, at Minnesota, U.S.A., served his apprenticeship to the printing business, about the year 1875, in "The Tyrone Constitution" then under the proprietorship of the late Mr. Nathaniel Carson, who died in 1895. The late Mr. Leslie came to "The Tyrone Constitution" from Ballybay, Co. Monaghan, and after serving his apprenticeship went to a Dublin publishing house, and later emigrated to Minnesota, where he established the wholesale paper business, and had a very successful business career.

This is the first visit Mr. John C. Leslie has paid to Ireland. He travelled from the South to Belfast, where he met some cousins, and on Wednesday was on his way to Enniskillen and Lough Erne; but hoped to visit Ballybay, his father's native place, before returning to the South. He procured several copies of "The Tyrone Constitution" to take back with him to America.

Atlantic, with a few passengers and quite a load of proximity fuses, destined for Loch Neagh, near Belfast, Northern Ireland — a combat zone.

When we landed that night we were informed that the first V-1's or 'buzz-bombs' had fallen on London. Quite an interesting prospect, since I was going to London the next morning.

These weapons were rather nerve-racking and destructive, coming over London at random, both day and night. When the putt-putt engine stopped, you knew that some 2,200 lb. of TNT was going to land in your vicinity quite soon. I remember one mid-day at our office at 17 Pall Mall, when this occurred, followed shortly by a tremendous explosion. That was when the upper floors of the Regent Palace Hotel at Piccadilly Circus were hit.

Another dark midnight, I was walking up from the Savoy Hotel to the Ritz feeling very isolated because all of the front vestibules and areaway gates were locked. There was no place to take refuge except in the gutter, but happily, no buzz bomb found me that night. Later on, the Germans began pumping the V-2's, the real rockets, into London, but I never was there at the time.

In questioning my friends about the effect of the one versus the other on the population, it developed that the women disliked the V-1 the most, but the men disliked the V-2. In the case of the women, it was the apprehension of waiting for that engine to stop. In the case of the men it was wondering whether that loud explosion in the distance was in the region of your family home.

Boeing 314 in warpaint at LaGuardia

Leslie's travel logs show that he spent at least 15 percent of the war years in Africa and Europe. In one mission he was gone for 60 days. There is very little information on these trips, some do not appear at all, but we know about them. For example, when he flew President Roosevelt to Africa for the Casablanca Conference, there is no contemporary record in his papers. For others the information is partial. It is likely we will never know completely where he went or for what reason.

Yankee Clipper at Foynes, about 1940

Capetown Clipper in warpaint

John Leslie with Chief Pilot Harold Gray.

Leslie and New York City Mayor William O'Dwyer, left, who held the rank of Brigadier General during the war

"WE ARE ALL FIGHTING WITH ONE MIND AND HEART"

From Leslie's memoirs:

In January 1943 I was given what I suppose was my major assignment in the war. It was to organize President Roosevelt's trip to Casablanca in two of our big Boeing flying boats. As a Naval Reserve officer, I got a call from a friend on active duty who said I'd better come down to Washington and discuss certain matters. When I got there, I was told what was afoot, obviously in the utmost secrecy.

When I returned to LaGuardia, I quietly arranged for two Boeing B-314 aircraft to be available on the designated day. I looked at the duty schedule of our captains, to see who would be available when needed. I was determined that I should not make a 'special selection' to fly the President of the United States, this on the grounds that all of my captains were fully qualified for that purpose, and there was no way of distinguishing one from another. It happened that the captains next in line were Howard Cone and Richard Vinal, both graduate aeronautical engineers. In sequence, Cone was to pilot the President's plane and Vinal the second plane on which the most of the rest of us would ride for the entire journey.

I left New York with two big flying boats without anybody else knowing where we had gone. Certainly, I told my wife that I could not even suggest where I was going, or how long I'd be there, but if she watched the papers she might be able to guess. We flew the two ships to Miami and tied them up at opposite sides of the Pan Am terminal at Dinner Key.

I was instructed to report to the office of the Rear Admiral commanding the local Naval District. Then I returned to the flight office at Dinner Key where the passenger list and the other ship's papers were being prepared. I recall the cold blue fluorescent light, the atmosphere heavy with cigarette smoke, and Captain Cone coming up to look at the passenger list. He found listed as number one a 'Mr. Jones.'

He began to speculate out loud as to who that could be, such as Jesse Jones of the Reconstruction Finance Corporation. Not until he walked down to his aircraft to see the preparations made for boarding the President did he realize what his assignment was.

Nor did I realize until that time how severely handicapped the President was. There had to be a special ramp from the dock to the aircraft and he had to be carried into the passenger cabin.

The trip from Miami to first overnight stop in Port of Spain, Trinidad was uneventful. The next day we flew from Port of Spain to Belem, Brazil, to refuel and then take-off at night for the trip across the South Atlantic to Bathurst, British Gambia. There the USS Memphis was waiting to accommodate the President and all the rest of us.

Clipper One with FDR aboard alighting alongside the USS Memphis at Bathhurst, by Ian Marshall

From Leslie's 1972 speech at Phillips Exeter Academy:

I have only one more tale and that is about the time we took President Roosevelt, in total secrecy, to North Africa for the Casablanca Conference in January 1943. This was the first time that a President of the United States had ever flown while in office and the first time that a President of the United States had left the country in time of war.

We used two Pan Am Boeing Clippers that were under the wartime control of the US Navy. The two Pan Am captains and I had long been Naval Reserve officers and were called to active duty for this particular project. Skipping the details, I want to leave you with a picture of President Franklin Delano Roosevelt at Bathurst, British Gambia, in West Africa. Upon our arrival, the President was taken on a boat tour of the harbor (with the rest of us in other small boats astern.)

I will always remember the picture of the President's boat coming alongside the USS Memphis and its being hoisted aboard in the setting sun. Like the Navy man he was, the President, sitting in the stern of his open boat, turned toward the U.S. flag at the stern of the Memphis and placed his white Panama hat over his breast as he came over the side. This was not done for press photographers; there were none!

*In this **very** remote quarter of the earth, at a fearsomely dangerous phase of a World War, bearing the lonely burden of defending his country against Hitler and Japan, there he was saluting the flag of his country in the time-honored fashion of the United States Navy.*

Leslie's memoirs continue:

The President continued his journey from Bathurst to Casablanca in a Douglas C-54 piloted by Otis Bryan of TWA. We sat out the ten days of the conference very comfortably aboard the Memphis. When the President returned to Bathurst after the conference, it was planned that he should go to Fisherman's Lake, Liberia to have a brief meeting with the Liberian President. From there we were to take off from that nicely-protected water direct to Natal. To my consternation, word reached me from the President's group on the other side of the lake that he had decided to fly back to Bathurst, have dinner there, then take off from Bathurst to Natal at midnight.

I had utterly no way of reaching anybody to advise against this procedure but it made me very anxious indeed to think of using that big Gambia River at night. We could have no patrolled area, no adequate lighting, no protection against either driftwood or native boats.

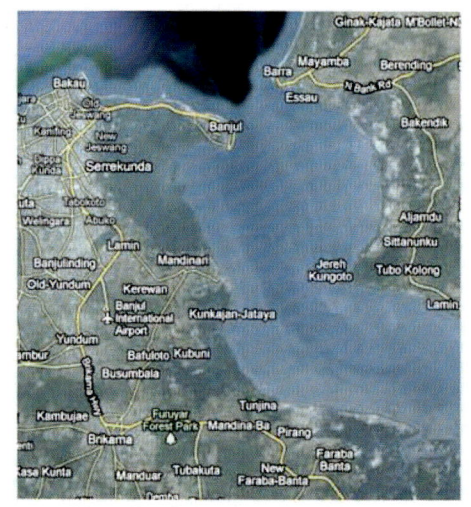

Mouth of the Gambia River, Bathhurst

Had I been in a position to do so, I would have attempted to veto the operation. This being impossible, we had to make the best of it. Captain Vinal and I decided that we would go down the river first and if there were any obstructions we would take the brunt. Then if we got off safely, the President's plane would follow close behind us.

I stationed myself in the top of the wing at the navigator's astrodome for our take-off, watching anxiously over the tail of our ship for the running lights that would indicate the following plane was safely in the air. My relief when I saw them was unlimited. (Leslie inserted here in handwriting *'As I write this I wonder whether we used any running lights at all or whether we were blacked out even for take off.'*)

The rest of the trip home was uneventful. Preparing for the final day's flight from Trinidad to Miami, on the President's birthday, we got a nice birthday cake for him and 'dressed' the aircraft with signal pennants which read 'Happy Birthday, Chief.'

The president cuts his birthday cake. Admiral Leahy awaits a slice.

Leslie offered this airborne toast to the president on his birthday.

> "Passengers and crew of Clipper No. 2 request you to inform the President that they will drink to his health and happiness at 1620 GMT, wishing him many happy returns of his birthday. That our Commander-in-Chief should for the first time be celebrating his birthday in the vast freedom of the sky seems to us symbolic of the new day for which we are all fighting with one mind and heart."

Before reaching Miami, I went topside and dressed in my Navy blues, with stiff white collar, black tie, and grey gloves, fancying (correctly) this would be the appropriate thing to do at the end of such an historic journey. When I sought out my local superior, the Chief of Staff of the Naval District, to report in, he paid me a compliment which would only have significance to one who appreciated its meaning. He said 'Welcome back, Commodore.' This was the courtesy title for any officer in command of two or more vessels, however small or however airborne.

From Miami I went back to Washington to report completion of the assignment and for a welcome reunion with my wife. I was alternating constantly for a day or two between appointments requiring naval uniform and those requiring civilian clothes so that she and I were going up and down the elevators of the Mayflower Hotel with me looking quite different from hour to hour. She finally protested that her reputation simply couldn't stand this performance any longer.

Leslie framed the letter of thanks he received from the President and mused in later years that a decision he made in a few seconds to call his two planes *Clipper One* and *Clipper Two*, rather than their Pan Am names, *Dixie Clipper* and *Atlantic Clipper*, entered the American lexicon with a sense of majesty and power as AIR FORCE ONE. He recalled the debriefing at which he was asked what call signs he used. He replied, "I just called them One and Two." Presidential flights ever since have been "ONE" for the President and "TWO" for the backup plane or for the Vice President.

This letter from President Roosevelt hung in Leslie's office.

THE WHITE HOUSE
WASHINGTON

February 19, 1943

Dear Commander Leslie:

I want to send you and the crews of Clipper "Number One" and Clipper "Number Two" this personal note to tell you how very much I appreciate your generous contribution to the National Foundation for Infantile Paralysis.

I want to tell you, too, what a wonderful trip I had and how much I enjoyed it. The arrangements were perfect and I did not have an uncomfortable moment.

With my grateful thanks to you for the fine service which you rendered and with every best wish to you all.

Very sincerely yours,

Franklin D. Roosevelt

Lieutenant Commander John C. Leslie, USNR,
Pan American Airways System,
Miami,
Florida.

"WIN THE WAR AND THE FUTURE!"

The war still had more than a year to go before it was over, but John Leslie was already asking Atlantic Division to make a final push so that prosperity for all would return with peace. He wrote short messages to staff in most division newsletters.

Division Manager Leslie Says:

WIN THE WAR — AND THE FUTURE

"All of us these days feel that our first and foremost job is winning the war — and none of us would let anything interfer with that. We want to make certain that we have won the war in order to have a better America in the future. In ordinary language, that means that we want to do everything we can to make certain that there will be jobs for the veterans when they return from the armed forces, and that there will be steady jobs and promotions for all of us as well. In the case of the overseas airline business, we have a still further aim: we want to do everything we properly can to make certain that the American flag will always have its proper share of the international airline business, and will never virtually disappear, as did the American merchant marine."

Sadly, right after Leslie's return from the flawless presidential flight, in February, 1943, veteran pilot Rod Sullivan, alighting on the Tagus River, Lisbon, crashed the *Yankee Clipper* with 24 fatalities.

Leslie wrote:

> *Of course, not all was successful on the Atlantic Division during the war. Particularly doleful was our loss of the Yankee Clipper on the Tagus River in Lisbon as one of our most experienced captains was landing at dusk. The assumption is that he made a descending turn into the landing area and in the poor visibility the left wing tip hit the water which broke up the airplane. The captain and many passengers survived, but he resigned his hard-earned position as a very senior Pan Am captain.*

Pictured in happier times are VP Sam Pryor, Captain Rod Sullivan, Mr. Trippe, and Leslie. The navigator's astrodome from which Leslie anxiously watched Clipper One follow his Clipper Two is visible atop the wing of the B-314.

The war ended in the summer of 1945 and the transition to peace time operations began. In 1945 John Leslie was elected Vice President and in 1946 transferred to the company headquarters in New York City.

Leslie bid a grateful farewell to his fellow employees in the Atlantic Division. They had shared in a great effort and they had prevailed. Now they could look to a better tomorrow

Leslie's 15 year service pin

No single image evokes better the past glory and pioneering of America's merchant marine and the comparable role of Pan American's flying boats than this painting by Gordon Grant, 'Yankee Clippers Sail Again.'

ATLANTIC DIVISION
Volume 5

J. C. Leslie Lauds Atlantic Division In Parting Message

TO MY FRIENDS IN THE ATLANTIC DIVISION

I wish that I could say *au revoir* to each of you individually before moving from the Division to the System Executive Office.

We have been through a great deal together since I came to the Atlantic almost six years ago. Most importantly, we have fought a war together, with all its mixture of high purpose, personal sacrifice, economic dislocation, general stress and strain. You can be proud of our record while in war service for the Navy and Army Air Transport Services.

During the past year we have been swinging back into our real reason for being: peaceful international air transport. Great decisions have been made affecting, for better or worse, not only our Company, but American aviation as a whole. We have made the transition from seaplanes to landplanes; we have prepared for vital new routes; we have had the long-awaited opportunity to initiate more efficient and profitable methods of operation and sales promotion.

During all these years I have been blessed with your friendship and support. Whatever we have accomplished has resulted from your ability, your hard work, and your team-play. I am deeply grateful; I can only say "thank you," from the bottom of my heart.

Sincerely,
JOHN C. LESLIE.

EPILOGUE

Jean and John Leslie at La Guardia Airport, 1949

The dramatic pioneering days were over. Planes were being manufactured in the hundreds and thousands, rather than single digits or, at most, dozens. The flying boat was replaced by the landplane. Air travel would become a commodity, taken for granted in the developed world like electricity, heating, air conditioning, and running water. Airlines would be regulated as public utilities. The Pan Am story would continue to be compelling, but in a different way. The next phase would be the rapid expansion of routes, equipment and personnel. Pan American would become not only "The World's Most Experienced Airline," but also the biggest.

For John Leslie a third career was starting. He now tackled policy, strategy, routes and regulation. He believed "air transportation is a public utility and can only survive in a regulatory regime," and that was the case until the Airline Deregulation Act of 1978.

John Leslie was elected to the board of directors in 1950. Many observers thought at the time and subsequently that he was being groomed to be Juan Trippe's successor.

This teletype message, shown here in part, announced the promotion to Pan Am offices around the world and was also released to the press.

```
AT A MEETING OF THE BOARD OF PAN AMERICAN WORLD AIRWAYS
JOHN C LESLIE VICE PRESIDENT HAS BEEN ELECTED A DIRECTOR OF THE
COMPANY IT WAS ANNOUNCED TODAY JUAN T TRIPPE.

EFFECTIVE JUNE 1 VICE PRESIDENT LESLIE HAS ALSO BEEN APPOINTED
VICE PRESIDENT-ADMINISTRATION SUCCEEDING THE LATE HOWARD B DEAN

AS DIVISION ENGINEER FOR THE PACIFIC DIVISION IN 1935 HE
DEVELOPED THE ENGINEERING TECHNIQUE FOR LONG RANGE FLIGHT WHICH MADE
POSSIBLE THE FIRST COMMERCIAL AIR SERVICE ACROSS THE PACIFIC.
SUBSEQUENTLY HE WAS OPERATIONS MANAGER OF THE PACIFIC DIVISION.
DURING THE WAY HE MANAGED THE COMPANYS ATLANTIC DIVISION WHERE HE WAS
RESPONSIBLE FOR PAN AMERICANS EXTENSIVE WARTIME OPERATIONS TO
EUROPE AND AFRICA. IN 1945 HE WAS MADE VICE PRESIDENT IN CHARGE
OF THE ATLANTIC DIVISION AND IN AUGUST 1946 HE WAS TRANSFERRED TO
MR TRIPPES STAFF AT SYSTEM HEADQUARTERS IN NEW YORK.
```

The company masthead in its 1950 annual report showed Leslie's name near the top.

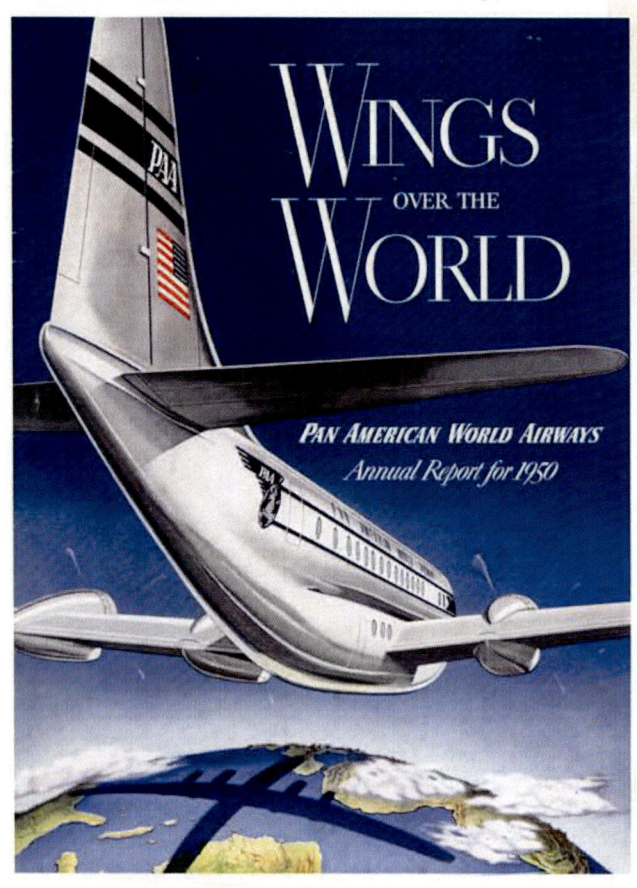

Leslie's 20 year pin.

PAN AMERICAN WORLD AIRWAYS, INC.
135 E. 42 St., New York 17, N.Y.

DIRECTORS

Harold M. Bixby*	Robert Lehman
S. M. Fairchild	John C. Leslie
Robert V. Fleming	E. O. McDonnell*
Henry J. Friendly	Mark T. McKee*
Franklin Gledhill	Samuel F. Pryor*
Merrill Griswold	W. H. Standley
David S. Ingalls	Vernon F. Taylor
J. T. Trippe*	

SYSTEM EXECUTIVE OFFICERS

President	J. T. Trippe
Vice-President and Asst. to President	Samuel F. Pryor
Vice-President	John C. Leslie
Vice-Pres. and General Counsel	Henry J. Friendly
Vice-President	E. Balluder
Vice-President	Franklin Gledhill
Vice-President	Harold M. Bixby
Vice-President	John H. Towers
Vice-President—Traffic and Sales	Willis G. Lipscomb
Vice-President and Chief Engineer	A. A. Priester
Comptroller	J. S. Woodbridge
Treasurer	R. G. Ferguson
Secretary and General Attorney	H. Preston Morris
Vice-Pres.—Latin American Div.	Wilbur L. Morrison
Vice-Pres.—Pacific-Alaska Div.	Harold E. Gray
Vice President—Atlantic Division	Harold R. Harris
Vice-President	Clarence M. Young

Shortly after his promotion in 1950, John Leslie was stricken with a virulent case of polio, which paralyzed him almost entirely from the neck down. For months he hovered near death in an iron lung.

Charlie Trippe, Juan Trippe's son, recalls sitting with his mother while his father went to see John Leslie. His mother explained to him the sad reality of polio, which was sweeping the nation in that year, and how distressed her husband was by his colleague's illness.

Mr. Trippe told John and Jean that his job was waiting for him when he recovered. There is no doubt this made an enormous difference in Leslie's recovery and return to work. That return would not be fully accomplished for a year. During that time Juan Trippe bolstered Leslie's morale immeasurably. He asked asked him to edit the annual report at home, to review other important documents, and he invited Jean Leslie to come on the next director's trip, which she did. Bit by bit John Leslie returned to work and at the end of a year was working full time.

PAN AMERICAN WORLD AIRWAYS SYSTEM

CHRYSLER BUILDING, 135 EAST 42ND STREET, NEW YORK 17, N. Y.

OFFICE OF THE
PRESIDENT

January 17, 1951

Mr. John C. Leslie
8 Murray Hill Road
Scarsdale, New York

Dear John:

I am enclosing a copy of the detailed itinerary of the Directors' inspection trip next month, which, as you remember, was discussed at the last Board meeting.

Even though you may not feel equal to making the trip yourself, I wanted you to know that we would be delighted to have Jean accompany the party.

If she decides to go, please let me know, and we will be glad to assist in connection with visas, and so forth, and in every other way.

Sincerely,

Juan

Above: Juan Trippe and John Leslie, 1950

Left: Jean Leslie disembarks at a stop during the 1951 Director's Trip

Betty Trippe, Juan's wife, wrote this in her "Diary and Letters:"

John Leslie, a graduate of Princeton and M.I.T., started out with Pan Am as a young engineer. At the age of forty-eight, he came down with polio and was not able to return to work for a year. Juan kept him on as Vice President and reassured him that his job was waiting for him. Dr. Howard Rusk said that knowing his job was waiting for him was in great measure responsible for his recovery. Although severely crippled, John Leslie was in a wheel chair and flew all over the world. He represented the company at the meetings of the International Air Transport Association. He was a brilliant administrator and was one of the important dedicated men who shared the belief in the future of aviation. I always felt that Juan had it in the back of his mind that John Leslie might succeed him as President, but, of course, due to his illness, he could not have assumed this great responsibility.

John Leslie returned to work a quadriplegic and was confined to a wheel chair. He could not not lift a glass to his mouth nor could he eat without a special device, nicknamed "the worker," which he designed and that Pan Am mechanics manufactured. He drank from a silver straw, many of which were presents from airline colleagues in Latin America. He could, however, roll his arm across the desk, grasp a pen to write and slide papers around. He used a speaker phone operated by buttons his fingers could reach.

The Economist commented on Leslie's polio

Juan Trippe started what became Pan American World Airways when he was 28 and had $300,000 ; long before that he had been running charter services. He retired this week at 68 with his reputation for shrewdness and driving efficiency as high as it has ever been. Pan Am is difficult to imagine without him. He might have withdrawn earlier from the active running of the airline (until this week he was still chief executive), had he not had exceptionally bad luck in choosing a successor. One of his heirs apparent, John Leslie, was cruelly incapacitated with polio just at the time of his promotion ;

Left: Leslie's pivoting "worker" that enabled him to bring food to his mouth.

Right: Leslie asked people to reach out and shake his hand. Note also his silver straw.

The Leslies and James Jones are greeted by Pan Am staff in Manila

Crucial to his recovery was his loving, dedicated, courageous and resourceful wife, Jean. Their children remember her motto, "Make it look easy." She wanted John to appear to live a normal life even though he did not. Children and staff learned to be alert to needs as they arose and to deal with them discretely. A glass would be refilled, food prepared, a pipe lighted or anything else. It was all done with hardly a word spoken. Always Jean hovered nearby on their many trips abroad, ready to solve any problems, always the gracious hostess or guest.

Many individuals were instrumental in John Leslie's rehabilitation, but James Jones, his wheel chair attendant, deserves special mention. He was a gardener and handyman when Leslie contracted polio. While he had little formal education, he had risen to sergeant in US Army. He served in the Pacific during the war, including at Guadalcanal. As he traveled around the world with Leslie, James became popular with officials and their employees no matter what differences of language, race, or position might exist. When a group photograph was taken he would place Leslie's wheelchair and attempt an exit. An airline president or high ranking official would often grab his arm and say, "No, James, you belong with us."

Leslie and Jones shelter in the shade of a DC6 somewhere in Africa or the Middle East

Leslie and Jones at an IATA- International Air Transport Association meeting

Pan American 1954 Directors's Trip to the Bahamas, Juan Trippe at far right, the Leslies toward the left.

IATA Executive Committee meets Irish President de Valera at the Presidential Residence, 1962

Leslie's service pins for 25, 30, 35, and 40 years

The Medicare Bill, 1965

Leslie's pioneering was not restricted to aviation. His children were surprised to find in his papers a letter from the White House sending him one of the pens used by President Johnson to sign the Medicare Bill in 1965.

They knew he had served as Chairman of the Committee on Aging of the Community Service Society of New York, but they had no recollection of his having served on the national, bipartisan committee that crafted a program that would cover seniors and that would ultimately be enacted by Congress and signed by the president.

President Johnson used 72 pens to sign the landmark Medicare Bill. Presumably, 12 went to the members of the committee Leslie served on. The other 60 probably were given to members of Congress who served on the committees involved in crafting the final legislation.

The creation of Medicare took years of debate, often acrimonious. Many said it could not be done; others said it should not be done. Most despaired that it ever would be done.

There is an uncanny parallel to the days when aviation's pioneers dreamed that oceans could be crossed by flying machines carrying, mail, people and cargo. Most thought it was technically impossible, perilous, and of no economic value.

Pioneering can take place anywhere: in a test tube, in the air, and even in the halls of Congress.

Leslie's innate modesty about his accomplishments left even his own children in the dark.

He was, indeed, a "quiet pioneer."

THE WHITE HOUSE
WASHINGTON

August 2, 1965

Dear Mr. Leslie:

The President has asked me to send you the attached pen used when he signed H. R. 6675, the Medicare Bill.

With best wishes,

Sincerely,

Lawrence F. O'Brien
Special Assistant
to the President

Mr. John C. Leslie
Chairman, Committee on Aging
Community Service Society
  of New York
New York, New York

A NATIONAL PROGRAM FOR FINANCING HEALTH CARE OF THE AGED

Guiding Principles
for
Complementary
Public and
Private Action

A Report to the American Public from the
NATIONAL COMMITTEE ON HEALTH CARE OF THE AGED

Summing Up

In the summer of 1952 Leslie gave the keynote address at a gala Pan American family picnic at the World's Fair Aquashow Amphitheater in New York. The occasion was to celebrate the company's 25th anniversary and the premiere of a movie, *New Horizons*, about the company's storied history. The overflow crowd of about 9,000 was entertained by Fred Waring and his Pennsylvanians and by an aqua show. Company morale could not have been higher.

Introducing the film, Leslie summed up the flying boat period with the phrase, "Call it Romance, if you will..." The crowd broke into a spontaneous roar of applause. In the 1920s, 30s and 40s roars of applause for Pan American flying boats echoed around the world.

Later the applause was for the airline's war effort, then for a string of firsts; among the many, the inauguration of jets culminating in the majestic Boeing 747, a worthy successor to the mighty Boeing B-314.

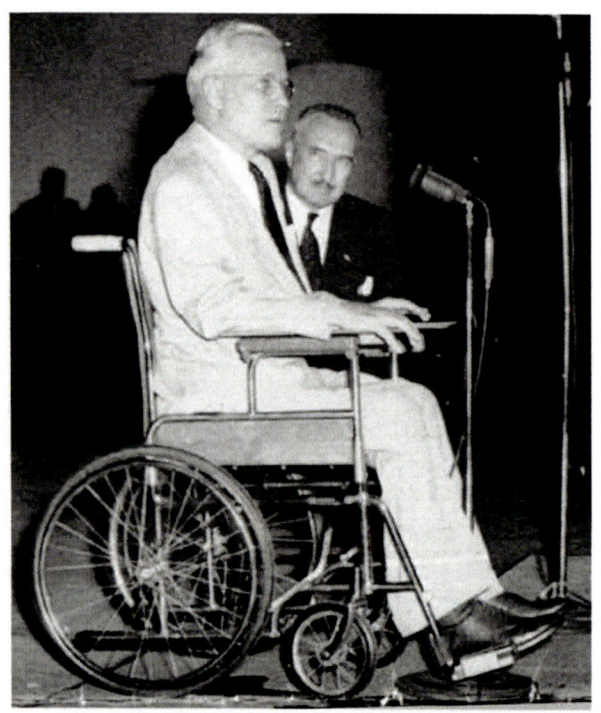

Pan Am Vice Presidents Leslie and Harris addressed the crowd.

PAA Personnel See "New Horizons" In New York, Mia, SFO

A total of 12,000 PAA personnel and their families crowded in recent weeks into amphitheaters, auditoriums and hangars in New York, Miami and San Francisco to see the premiere of "New Horizons", the film story of PAA's growth from a single route charter to world-girdling airways.

Call it Romance, if you will....
John Leslie, 1952

FINAL FLIGHTS

John Leslie retired in 1970 after a 42 year career, but continued to work at the Pan Am Building on the Pan Am History Project. The first Pan Am Historical Foundation was formed in 1975 and Leslie continued historical research until 1979.

All told, his years with Pan Am spanned half a century.

He and Jean retired to their hilltop home in Antigua, West Indies, an island they had first visited on a Sikorsky S-38 during the 1930 honeymoon trip described in this book.

He died peacefully in 1982, in the arms of his beloved Jean, on their terrace overlooking one of the vast oceans he and fellow pioneering aviators challenged and conquered so many years earlier.

AFTERWORD

As I read my father's papers I was struck by the vision, the Herculean effort, and the logistics that went into the earliest airmail and passenger transoceanic flights. I was also struck by the risks these pioneers knew they were taking and what they did to minimize them.

I did not find as much as I expected about the loss of two Clippers in the Pacific and one in the Atlantic. My father knew the pilots and crews well, some as close friends. He and his team had planned the flights, prepared the ships to fly and one would explode in mid-air, the second would disappear without a trace, while the third was lost by pilot error.

I do know, however, the memory of those disasters stayed with him because one day, when my business career had suffered a setback, I sought his advice at his office in the Pan Am Building. He listened and said, "Your losses can be measured in time and money; there are much more terrible ways." Then tears welled up in his eyes and he looked away from me, out over the towers of Manhattan to the horizon. I could almost see in his mind's eye the silver speck of a Clipper disappearing over the horizon, a flying boat lost in the vast ocean. He would still cry more than thirty years later.

I had the privilege of working for Pan American during three summers while in college, first on mid-Pacific Canton Island refueling and servicing the Boeing Stratocruisers going to Australia. Every midnight we boarded a boat and cruised across the lagoon from the old seaplane base to the landing field. I have never forgotten the romance of that work, the pilot's voice coming over the PA system, "Island in sight."

I worked in Brussels selling tickets and checking in passengers. I learned important diplomatic skills weighing not only the luggage, but also the passengers. My final summer was in Bogota, Colombia, working for Pan Am affiliate, AVIANCA. For a language major these jobs were wonderful and I was proud to wear the Pan Am uniform. I still have my winged globe pin and my cap insignia.

Author en route to Brussels on a DC-6 freighter, 1955

Peter Leslie, Waterford, Maine, 2011

ACKNOWLEDGMENTS, WITH THANKS

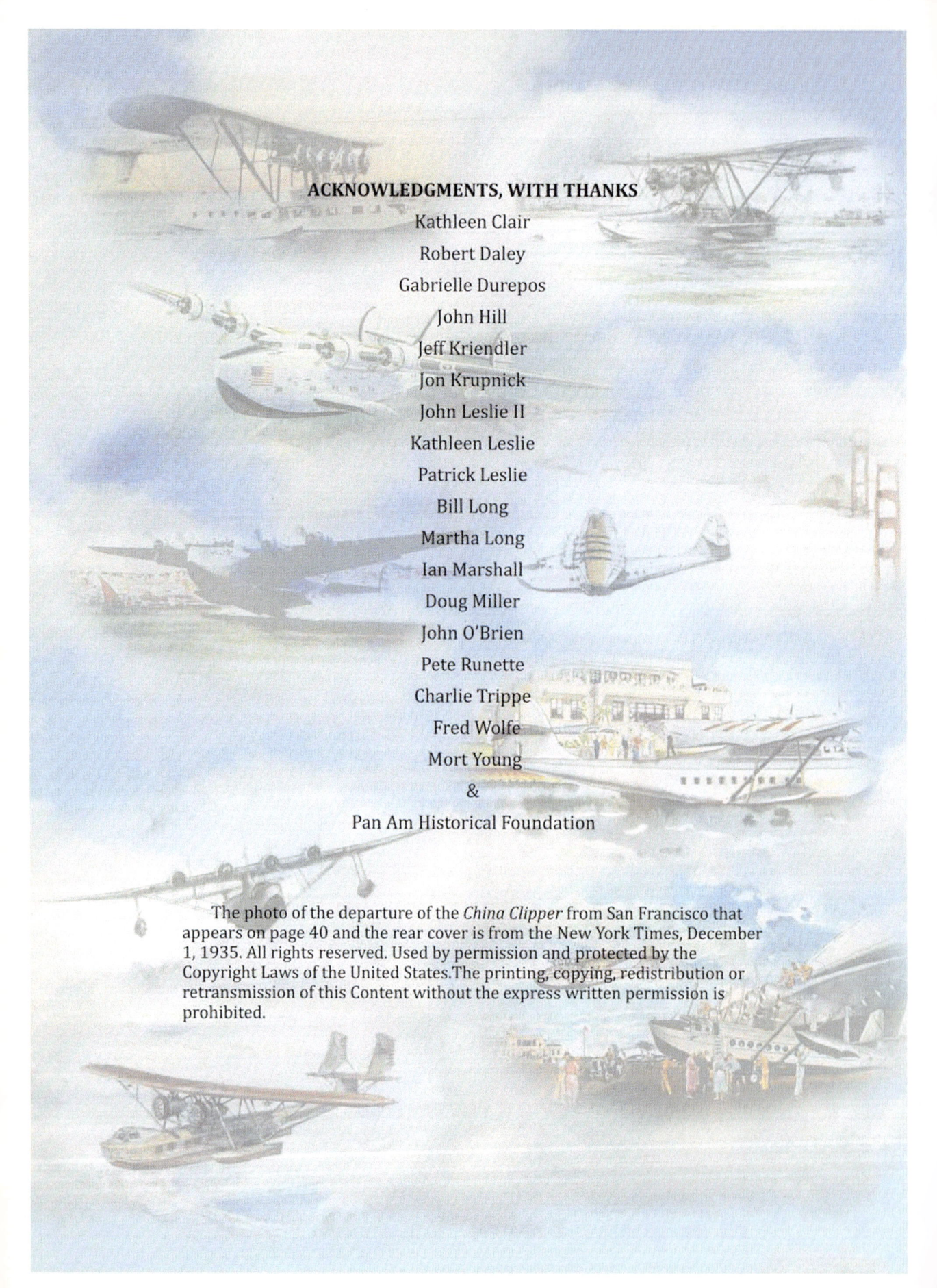

Kathleen Clair

Robert Daley

Gabrielle Durepos

John Hill

Jeff Kriendler

Jon Krupnick

John Leslie II

Kathleen Leslie

Patrick Leslie

Bill Long

Martha Long

Ian Marshall

Doug Miller

John O'Brien

Pete Runette

Charlie Trippe

Fred Wolfe

Mort Young

&

Pan Am Historical Foundation

The photo of the departure of the *China Clipper* from San Francisco that appears on page 40 and the rear cover is from the New York Times, December 1, 1935. All rights reserved. Used by permission and protected by the Copyright Laws of the United States. The printing, copying, redistribution or retransmission of this Content without the express written permission is prohibited.